DEDICATION

———

TO MY HUSBAND, JOE

Thank you for loving me through the long process of this book. From the early morning hours to the late evening writings, you were so patient in helping me pour my heart onto paper, and taking my words and making them come alive. Because of you, this assignment was able to be fulfilled, and I am forever grateful. You truly do make me the best I can be.

I would also like to thank my many friends and family who lived this with me, and then stood beside me and encouraged me to get this story out. I love you all!

A JOURNEY WITH GOD TO HEAR HIS VOICE
AND EXPERIENCE THE BIG & MORE

JUST SHOW UP

MISTY STINSON

WHEN WRITING THIS BOOK

———

I realized it was quite the challenge to write about individuals involved in my life story without possibly tapping into extremely personal areas of their lives.

On one hand, I knew that I had to present complete truth; on the other, I knew this could cause possible discomfort to some. In one instance the individual had passed so I felt uncomfortable using their name without their consent.

The solution I chose was to rename certain individuals to preserve their privacy. I also chose to use first names only throughout the book and leave out certain specific locations.

Please be assured that other than these minor changes everything in this book is told exactly as it happened.

JUST SHOW UP
MISTY STINSON

For additional information and to
order copies of this book, visit
MistyStinson.com

COVER AND INTERIOR DESIGN:

Sana Branding + Marketing

PUBLISHED BY:

Ripples Press

Paperback ISBN: 979-8-9870176-2-3

TABLE OF CONTENTS

ENDORSEMENTS

I have one word for this book: enthralling. Misty takes you on a tour of her own spiritual journey in a humble and transparent way. I felt I was on "HOLY GROUND" as Misty unfolded her very "real and personal" relationship with God. The range of topics is fascinating, and her convictions will challenge you to search for more from the Father, and the Son and especially the Holy Spirit. Read it with an open heart and perhaps you might hear the voice of God calling.

Jerry van Dalen
Pastor, Miami FL

. . . .

It is with great honor that I've been asked to write an endorsement for this amazing book. Misty's life story is truly one of testings, faith, breakthroughs, and triumph! Misty truly hears from God and knows how to activate what she hears. As a result, scores of lives have been impacted and set free! Read Misty's book, but let it also read you!

Leanne Goff
Founder and President, Leanne Goff Ministries
Author: *A Christian Life Without Father God*
& A Journey To Your Identity

I would describe Misty's life as an illuminated and living invitation to "Just Show Up!" So much of the "Big and More" in my own life can be traced back to my path intersecting with hers. It is my prayer that no matter how this book has ended up in your hands that you consider it an illuminated invitation to "Just Show Up!" and experience your own journey!

Pamela Christopher

The Resting Place Tampa

. . . .

Misty has unveiled her life of struggles and victories from valleys to mountain tops. Her simple honesty expresses her journey with passion. Once I started reading it, I just could not put it down. You, like me, will find your own journey on the pages of her book. She writes with the same enthusiasm that sparks her own love of life. Thank you Misty for moving us all forward with new hope.

Dr. Jerry Brandt

Founder and President, Kingdom Life University

Author: *I Am Who You Say I Am: Believe it! Declare it!*

CHAPTER 1

FROM THE BEGINNING...

I was in Chicago recently, talking to a lady I had never met. Our paths crossed in an airport, and while we sat and waited we were swapping stories. So it must have been my turn, and I was blabbering on, when all of a sudden she stopped me and asked, "How do you do that?"

"How do I do what?"

"How do you hear God's voice?"

I had been relating recent things going on, and hadn't even realized I was saying "God told me this" and "God told me that."

She continued, "I've been a Christian for a long time, but He doesn't tell me things. Or at least...not like that. Not like what you're describing."

So I thought about it, and before I answered her, I asked God, *Where do you want me to start?*

He plainly said, *From the beginning.*

And it hit me: *Oh, wow…that's huge.*

But it was exactly what needed to happen. So I took a deep breath, and went back to where it all started; and in the end, her eyes were opened in a way they wouldn't have been if I had jumped in somewhere in the middle. We were doing the ugly cry together, and hugging each other, and eventually she went her way and I went mine.

I know I will probably never see her again, but without a doubt I also know this: she got it.

She walked away from that meeting a different person than when we met. She had a fire in her eyes and a belief firmly planted in her heart that there was MORE.

And even though we only met in passing and haven't kept in touch, I trust God has radically changed her life. I choose to believe she went on to experience levels of freedom, and power, and love, and truth, and victory she had never known before.

My deepest desire for you is that in reading this book these same things and more will happen for you.

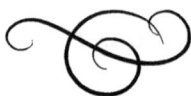

I was raised in Tennessee, on a farm in the country with my mom, dad, sister, dogs, cows, and horses. We had a huge garden with fresh veggies, and lots of hills and woods to play in. It was a beautiful area to live, with the front of our home looking out over the rolling hills of Starr Mountain, and a back yard of fields upon fields of pasture with a crooked little creek running through it. I spent many days playing silly kids' games like throwing a plastic bottle or stick in, and then running as fast as I could downstream to catch it as it went by. It was endless hours of good, healthy country living…mixed in with some hard work. After all, you can't have a farm without some farmhands!

Our small town had only a few red lights and one of them didn't actually work all the time, so I'm not really sure it counted. I would ride the school bus to school Monday through Friday, and go to church on Sunday morning, Sunday night, and Wednesday night. And whenever anything else was going on. That made up most of my schedule, most of my days.

It was a simple life, and so was my understanding of God. I knew Jesus died for me and God was His Father. I knew I had said the salvation prayer and was saved at Camp Cherokee, while I sat around a campfire with some of my church friends at the age of seven. Of course, I also remembered saying the prayer a number of other times over the years…you know, a little girl can never be too sure. I had a friend whose dad was a pastor and one time when I spent the night with her I said the prayer, as well as another time I was in church and my heart started racing when they did the altar call, and I felt like I should go forward. But as many times as I said "the prayer," for some reason I always had the question in my mind…*How do I know for sure?*

I did my best to read and learn the Bible. I learned about the Commandments, all eight of them…ha! I had you thinking you were going to have to put this book down already, didn't I? Stick with it, I think it'll be worth it. Anyway, I also learned all the things I was expected to do and not do in order to be a good girl. I loved being a part of the church, singing in the choir and going to all the youth group events. I truly tried my best to follow the rules because I knew they were supposed to be good for me.

So while I remember going to Sunday school and learning all the stories in the Bible, it seemed like I still didn't know how to bring church—or more correctly, God—into my everyday life. Having conversations about Jesus was not common for me at home or with my friends. Now if I was at church, we had conversations about the Bible, but the conversations stayed at church. In other words, I didn't necessarily "do" church when I was away from it.

Nevertheless, I was sure of one thing: God loved me. I may not have known the extent of it, but I did know He loved me.

I had that part down, but the rest seemed more difficult. How did I bring what I had inside church into my life away from church? It seemed like these were two separate lives that didn't always want to mash together. By the time I hit sixteen I tended to follow the rules less and less, and there became a growing distance between life inside church and life outside church. Looking back, I think of these as the "rough years," rather than rebellious, because I was never trying to shut God out. I was just trying to find happiness and fun, and I was looking in all the wrong places.

Even as my teenage life got complicated, my God remained pretty simple. For the most part He stayed in church, and life happened outside of church.

However, God did show up now and then in ways that were obvious and dramatic. There were certain events which I considered "God-moments." I knew the instant they happened that God was involved, and never questioned whether or not it was Him. In fact, there were two specific times when I know without a doubt death came for me, and except for the direct intervention and protection of our Heavenly Father, would have had me.

The first of these was a vicious dog attack. I was in the third grade, walking through our neighborhood, when out of nowhere a large dog rushed in front of me and started growling. Next thing I knew he had knocked me into a ditch and was on top of me. I just remember protecting my throat with everything I had. Somewhere in my young mind I understood that this animal was wanting to kill me. Miraculously, a neighbor named Mr. Rogers (seriously) heard my screams and ran out of his house and pulled the dog off.

By the time it was over I had deep bites on my shoulder, my stomach, and deep wounds on one of my thighs. I remember being in shock when they rushed me to the hospital. The recovery was extensive and very drawn out, and I am so grateful for my mom during this season, who sat right with me for many months helping me work through the different stages of infection, gangrene, slow healing, surgery, and eventual recovery from the painful injuries.

Finally, after more than six months, I had nothing left of the incident but some large scars and an even larger fear of dogs, which God and I work on to this day. I know in the depths of my being, without a doubt, that I was dead that day had God not used Mr. Rogers to step in and save me.

God also protected me one time when I was involved in a really nasty accident. Driving my boyfriend's Jeep, I lost control and slid off of a gravel mountain road. All I remember is trying to overcorrect the slide, which eventually sent us sailing over the edge of a cliff. The nose of the Jeep went down and I felt us flipping, several times nose over nose, and then several more times sideways on our way down the side of the mountain. Somewhere along the way I was thrown out, and when I came to I was lying on my back looking up at millions of stars in a beautiful night sky.

My boyfriend, however, ended up under the upside-down Jeep, pinned by the roll bar. I remember crying out for help at the top of my lungs. I don't know if I was crying to God, the stars, or just screaming, but I did know we were out in the middle of absolutely nowhere. It was late at night and very likely there was not another person around for many, many miles. But crazily enough, after only a few minutes I heard a voice yell back. We had wrecked close to an isolated lake where two men were camping, out on an island in the middle of the lake. They had heard the crash and jumped in their johnboat to come help.

It was pitch black, and they were coming as fast as their tiny motor would take them, which seemed like forever. Eventually, friends in another vehicle who had gone down the mountain some time ahead of us also came back searching. Together, with the help of strong logs and much muscle, they were all able to tilt the Jeep up and pull my boyfriend out. Thank goodness we were near a lake, because the mud helped save his life, allowing his body to sink just enough so the roll bar hadn't crushed him.

I can't even tell you to this day how we got back up the side of that mountain and into our friend's car, but the next thing I remember is waking up in the hospital. I never had the opportunity to thank the two men that helped rescue us that night but I'm forever grateful to them.

The Jeep, I saw later, had doors that looked like accordions. The steering wheel my hands had gripped was completely bent over, and the vehicle had obviously rolled many times. My boyfriend had bruised and bloody kidneys from being pinned down by the roll bar and took many weeks to recover, and I spent an extended time in and out of the hospital, having my spine poked and prodded and pulled and wearing a brace to get it back to a point the doctors were happy with. Again, my mother stayed right with me, completely setting her life aside to help me to heal, whatever that entailed. I remember telling her many times that it was almost like an angel had caught me in the air and laid me down on the side of the hill.

I understand life is full of circumstances, and circumstances can be unpredictable, but this was yet another time I knew God had directly intervened in my life. Our paths had crossed, and my life would be forever different than it otherwise would have been.

When I was nineteen I picked up and moved to West Palm Beach, Florida. Looking back I was so naive, so small-town… let's just say I kept God busy protecting me, more times and in more ways than I need to elaborate here. But the point is, again and again, there were "God-moments." Definite times I knew God stepped in and intervened. When the supernatural invaded the natural, if even for a moment. They were unmissable, and unmistakable, and undeniable.

In addition to times He protected me, I can also look back and see specific times when He comforted me, and provided for me. After five years in Florida, I got a call saying my father had been diagnosed with prostate cancer. I immediately packed up and moved back to Tennessee, wanting to be with him during this time. I was very fond of my father and not knowing what this cancer meant, I wanted to be close and spend as much time with him as I could.

My dad was a tough cookie. He had been through a lot in life and was a fighter, so when they gave him two years he stretched it out to ten. He and I ended up having some great times together and growing closer than ever. Talking with my father one day, I told him, "Dad, I just don't know if I'll ever find the one. I don't know if there's anyone out there I could spend my entire life with."

What a great time for a God-moment, right?

Within days of that conversation I walked into my Aunt Ginger's hair salon and met my future husband. Actually, he had come in for a haircut and she knew I was coming by, so she wouldn't let him out of the chair until I showed up! It's so good to have family watching out for you…

Anyway, he had just come up from Tampa, Florida to visit his parents who had retired and moved to the Tennessee mountains years earlier. His plans were to visit for a short time and then continue west to start a new job and new life. However, after we met, let's just say I did some rearranging on those plans and he ended up staying in our area a bit longer. In fact, until we got married six months later. Yes, you heard me....six months!

Joe was not only searching for the love of his life at this time (even if he didn't know it), he was also searching for something much bigger: his first love, God. When I met him, oh my goodness, did he have a lot of questions about God. God had been wooing him for some time and he was ready to hear answers. We had many conversations and during one special one with my dad, Joe gave his life to Jesus. It was such a sweet, sweet time, and yet another way God comforted and provided for me, because He knew how important it was to me for my future husband to know and love the Lord like I did.

So we were good to go! I was saved, my hubby was saved, we were married...I had it all covered!

Since my father was doing so well, Joe and I ended up moving back to Florida. A small town didn't supply jobs for the type of work Joe did and besides, my father had bought a motor home and loved coming down and spending time with us in the warm sunshine. Sometimes he would stay for a few months at a time, parked in our backyard or down in the Everglades hauling in what he swore were ten-pound bass.

And I guess it was right about then God started to stretch me. Joe and I moved into a townhome in West Tampa, and our next door neighbor was a sweet older lady who immediately invited us to church. Of course growing up Southern Baptist I loved church, and didn't really feel settled unless I was actively attending, so we were in. I was also pretty confident in what I would find there...I mean, church was church, right?

Well, the first time I walked into Tampa Covenant Church I knew something (other than the fact that it was non-denominational) was different. The music seemed to connect with me at a deeper place, and there was something special in the air, almost like electricity. And even more than that, there was this...joy...bursting out all over. I had never felt such a feeling of freedom, of being alive. People had their hands up in the air and were clapping, but not necessarily all together like it was planned out...more like something wonderful had ahold of them and they couldn't help it.

I realize to some of you that's probably not a big deal, but I remember thinking, *Really? You can do that?* The entire scene just made me smile.

Please understand, I loved my previous church. The people had become my best friends, and I'd learned a lot about the Bible there. But the atmosphere I was in now held a power, an attraction, a magnetism I hadn't felt before. There was a sense that while there was a definite program being followed, it could yield at any moment to whatever surprising thing God wanted to introduce.

Suffice it to say, this immediately became our new home church. Not only for the freedom of worship, but also for the depth of the teaching. This pastor was reading the same Bible, and preaching on the same verses, but it seemed like I had new ears. I was hearing things in a way I never had before, and seeing new connections between what the Word said and how it applied to real, everyday life. I just felt myself going so much deeper.

It was like the message, and the music, and the meaning held so much more. More life, more freedom, more joy. It surprised me, in such a good way. It felt like I had stumbled onto a real treasure.

CHAPTER 2

THE WAY HE MADE ME

Around this time I started a new bookkeeping job. Grammar has never been my favorite subject, nor writing, so if you take that into consideration you understand why I went with numbers. I loved to take all those seemingly disconnected dollars and make them fit together perfectly, down to the last penny. With no spelling involved it was fun, like a puzzle. Now, in my defense, it is true that in the hills of Tennessee we have a language all our own. I may not write with an accent, but if you heard me talk, you would say, "Yep. That girl's from Tennessee." So some of the words and expressions I consider normal just don't make sense in the outside world.

What I'm saying is I have a much better chance of getting the numbers right than getting the words right!

This particular company had a Bible study each Monday morning before work, and I decided to join. There were about ten of us on my first morning, and before we got started with the lesson the man leading the study said, "Let's go around the table and pray out loud, whatever God brings to you."

Oh, Holy Moly! I immediately started to get nervous, and couldn't stop thinking how unfair it was for him to just spring this on me like that. I had always hated to speak in public, and praying out loud was no exception. I was seated about number eight in the group of ten, so I tried to calm myself down and plan out what I would say when it came to be my turn. And don't you know as soon as I thought of something that seemed good, the very next person would say that exact thing! This happened three or four times, and each time I got a little more upset that this inconsiderate man would actually put me in such a position.

Well, when it came to be my turn, I was a wreck. I was all inside my head, way overthinking everything, and I just blurted out something very basic. I'm sure I was four shades of red, and sweating, and probably shaking. Immediately after the class I cornered this man...politely...and said, "I want you to know, I don't think it's right for you to ask people to pray out loud, in front of everyone. That's just not okay. Some of us have a hard time with that!"

The whole incident had rattled me so much I was just sure he was going to apologize, but instead he stood firm. He lovingly said, "I hear you, and I thank you, but this is how we do it here. I do hope you'll keep coming, and I hope you'll feel more comfortable next time."

Now, looking back on this, I laugh so hard! I'm grateful for this man's love, and patience. And his conviction to not budge on his beliefs, because God used him to confront a roadblock I had in my mind about praying out loud, in front of people. Of course I didn't know it at the time, but as long as I continued to give power to that lie, my future ministry could never be birthed.

But getting outside my comfort zone was not a normal thing for me. What if I didn't say the right thing? Up until that point, I hadn't really given God many opportunities to stretch me. Although I was always in Bible studies and church activities, I didn't ask myself to try anything crazy different. If this had not been the beginning of a new job around unfamiliar people, I more than likely would have just remained silent.

But as circumstances had it, I was put into a situation where I felt I had to push through the uncomfortable. And in the end I was better for it, even if I didn't realize at the time it was exactly what I needed in order to grow. While I never would have said so out loud, at that time I did think I had God and Christianity pretty much figured out. I understood God was Love, and Truth, and that Jesus was the only way to heaven. I also knew that even though God was always there, He only showed up personally during super-special "God-moments," and those didn't happen all that often.

It's probably correct to say I loved Him because I knew who He was and what He stood for rather than as a result of an actual personal relationship, like the way I loved my husband. And as big, and as powerful, and as capable as I knew God was, I evidently didn't think He was bigger than my fear of praying in public. Up until that point it had never even occurred to me to ask Him to change that within me…I just figured that's the way I was…that's the way He made me.

I remember one time my husband and I went to dinner at our new friends' house, Bob and Stephanie. We had just met them at Tampa Covenant Church, and two things stuck with me from this night: first, she served traditional spaghetti and tomato sauce… with salmon in it. I remember my poor husband, who's not much of a seafood eater, when he discovered the salmon (after he had put a heaping portion on his plate). His poor expression was…

What am I supposed to do now? I mean, there's just no way to rearrange that much spaghetti to make it look like you've actually eaten any of it.

The second thing came over dinner conversation, when I tried to explain to Stephanie this difficulty I had in reading the Bible. Beyond the fact that it was Aramaic, or Hebrew, or Greek translated into 15th century English (which isn't anything like Tennessee English) was the fact that sometimes, even when I understood all the words...it just didn't seem to make sense. Like it wouldn't open up for me. Without hesitation, Stephanie, who was very bold (bold enough to serve spaghetti with salmon in it) said, "Well, we just need to pray for that. Let's pray for God to give you understanding when you read the Bible."

My automatic response was, "Ooh, that sounds great," thinking we would get around to it. Maybe next week in church, or maybe after some preparation, or maybe we would all go home and pray about it that night, during our "prayer time." Honestly, I don't know what I was thinking, but I certainly wasn't expecting her to stand up right in the middle of dinner and say, "Let's do it!"

My husband, eager for any excuse to leave the table, was probably like, *Yes! Thank you Lord!*

But I was thinking, *Right now? Out loud, in front of everybody?*

And again, just like at the office, there was almost a panic sensation that came with it. There was a dread I was going to take something so personal—my prayer life—and bring it out in the open, in front of other people for them to examine. Like maybe my prayers wouldn't be good enough, or I would mess it up somehow. But I stood up with her, and the four of us linked hands, and Stephanie began to pray, with normal words that actually made sense. She prayed very directly, very specifically, very boldly…and out loud…for God to open my eyes and open my mind to reading the Bible, so that understanding His Word would come easy for me.

Believe it or not, this was a new thing for me. The idea prayer could be so…relevant. So specifically directed to change something about myself which I had believed was so fixed, so unchangeable. Again, I remember thinking, *You can do that?*

I prayed all the time, but nothing like that. My prayers seemed more like thank-you prayers, or praying-for-other-people prayers, or even begging prayers…not super specific, take-authority prayers done with confidence like she was doing. For some reason I had just accepted that Bible reading was difficult for me. Again, I figured if that's the way God made me, it was set in stone, and I didn't challenge it. It almost felt like I was telling God He had messed up if I wanted Him to change the way He made me. But that evening as I listened to Stephanie's boldness and directness, my eyes were opened to a new way of praying. It was the first taste I had of praying with authority.

And I liked it.

About this time, when the little box I kept God in was growing bigger by the day, something else happened. A revival came to town. Or, more correctly, a preacher came to town and a revival broke out. Anyway, it wasn't the kind of thing you could easily miss. We all heard about it, taking place in a huge church not too far away, and every few days word was coming back of incredible things happening. So naturally, we had to go. In fact if I remember correctly, Stephanie didn't give us a choice.

Now to this day I don't remember what the exact message

was, just that there was a lot of joy going on during the preaching. The entire atmosphere was one where people were happy, relaxed, and having a good time. It seemed like a true celebration.

During the service we attended, the preacher asked everyone to stand and hold hands, and then he swung his arm across a section of the audience. When he did this, two-thirds of the people just PLOP! fell flat down. He turned and swooped his arm across one side of the room and it was like a big invisible wave smacked the people, and down they went. Then he did the same thing across the back of the room and the same thing happened. It was quite amazing, until he swooped this big ol' wave in our direction, and it seemed like everyone around us went down… and my husband and I just stood there.

I remember the two of us, sticking up like flagpoles, looking at the audience. All the people on either side of us, including Stephanie and her husband, had been hit with this wave of whatever. I remember us looking at each other, and finally sitting down, and I remember it was very…awkward.

At this point I had such mixed emotions. Were all these people actually just hit with something? If so, why didn't it hit me? Were they just falling because they thought they were supposed to? Because I certainly wasn't going to do that! That's not even real!

But what if it was? What if it was real…and I just wasn't getting it? Was God mad at me?

Did He love them more?

There were so many thoughts running around in my head, and I just didn't understand. When the people around us got up, they were all talking about this incredible experience—one which I didn't have—and I just had to wonder…were they all being fake, or did I just miss it?

When it was winding down they announced that anyone who wanted additional prayer should line up out in the lobby. Our ride home lined up, so my husband and I lined up as well. The lobby was a hallway that encircled the building, and as the prayer team worked their way down the line, they would pray for people, touch people, and many of them, again, would fall back.

I could see them work their way down the line toward me, and I was already telling myself ahead of time I would not fall back unless it was real. I watched them approach, and watched people fall back, one after the next. I was so worked up and anxious by the time they got to me, that when their hands touched my forehead I was already arguing with myself...*Do I feel anything? Are they pushing? It feels like they're pushing! I don't want to fall if it's not real...*

In the end I just laid back, because it was easier than arguing with myself.

The lady right next to us was deaf, and when the prayer team laid hands on her she fell back. There was someone with her who told them she was deaf, and at that point the whole team came together and began to pray over her. They kept commanding, loudly, in the name of Jesus, for hearing to come. They would ask if she could hear, and she would shake her head no. Again they would pray, more forcefully, more commandingly. Every time they would ask her, she would motion no, she couldn't hear anything.

And I laid there thinking...*Y'all just stop it! You're yelling at this poor girl!*

I remember feeling sorry for her, because they were being so demanding about something she had no control over. It seemed like they were doing something that wasn't right, because it seemed offensive. And I'm telling you, they didn't stop. They just kept on and on, demanding, then asking, "Can you hear? Can you hear?"

I kept thinking *No, she doesn't hear. She's deaf. Leave the poor woman alone!*

But here's what was interesting: In the past, I had prayed for God to heal me when I was sick. Any other time, away from that situation if you had asked me whether God could heal, I would have said yes. If you would have told me this girl who was deaf went to a revival and they laid hands on her and she was healed, I would have praised God and been excited. But there was something right there in that moment...

Maybe it had to do with being confronted with all the other things going on that didn't make sense, things that weren't structured, things I couldn't easily understand or explain. I would have loved to witness that girl get her hearing back, but I guess I just didn't believe yelling at her was going to do anything but make her feel bad. And there was already so much going on that evening which didn't make sense that it actually scared me, to be truthful about it.

In the end, I didn't even wait around to see if the girl got her hearing back. I was frustrated, and confused, and had reached the end of my understanding. I left that revival more jumbled up than ever. I wasn't sure what was truth. What I did know was that the ones who seemed to receive something or get knocked down sure did seem to enjoy it. And in the middle of all the laughing there was my husband and I, wandering around staring, trying to figure it all out. I didn't know if it was real, or if I had just barely escaped a cult. Truly. I had no idea. What I did know was I loved Jesus, and if He was a part of this then I wished He would reveal it in some way.

I wished I could know for sure.

Back at our church people were fired up from the revival. It brought a passion into the people and they were using this voice of authority to pray for everything. One day I showed up really depressed after another round of bad news about becoming a mother. Joe and I had been trying to have children for years and had gone through a miscarriage, which made the doctors question whether a successful pregnancy was even possible. We had gone through several rounds of artificial inseminations, and had just received news that yet another one had failed.

When I came into the church, friends there noticed something was wrong—I just couldn't put on my happy face. I wanted to be a mother more than anything in my entire life. When I was younger and people would ask what my career was going to be, I would say "I'm going to be a Mom!"

When I told my friends I had just found out I wasn't pregnant, they suggested the whole church pray for me. Next thing I knew, I was up front and people were laying hands on me and doing that authority thing again. It went on for some time, and I must say it felt good to have that many people praying so strongly for the baby I so desperately wanted. After the prayer, after I thanked everyone, I started thinking back to the girl who couldn't hear and how those people had prayed with her.

What was the difference? I felt good about the people praying for me...why had I felt sorry for her?

One of my best friends was getting married the next month and we were busy planning, preparing and having showers for her. Since I hadn't had an insemination that month (we would usually skip a month or two in between tries) I wasn't really keeping up with the calendar like I normally did. Sitting at home one night after the wedding was all over, it occurred to me I hadn't been keeping track of the days, and when I started adding it up...holy smokes! It looked like...

An old pregnancy test I had at home came out negative, and I got a little upset. Well, maybe a lot...we won't talk about that. Nevertheless, I decided to buy a new test first thing in the morning, because when it came to having a baby, my hope didn't die easy. I guess you see where this is going...the very next Sunday in church, we were celebrating a baby! It took me days to come down from the clouds, and I called everyone I had known since first grade. It was one of the happiest times of my life!

God had come through again. He was showing me that prayers do matter, and they do create miracles. Once again, my mind went back to the deaf girl. Should I have been powerfully praying for her right alongside everyone else, rather than feeling sorry for her? There was no question in my mind that my baby was a direct answer to prayer. I thanked God that night that I had friends willing to pray for me with power and authority, rather than being worried about offending me.

Not long after that Stephanie let me know she was starting a women's prayer group at her house, and invited me to join. With all the uncertainty lately, one thing I did know was I was in love with God and wanted more of Him, so I immediately said yes. At the first meeting there were about eight women at Stephanie's house, and I knew most of them, at least casually. They either went to our church or I had met them at dinners, get-togethers, or whatever. The point is they were not strangers.

I don't remember what the actual Bible study was on...

definitely good stuff and something I was in favor of. As the group came together for the first time in her living room, Stephanie said "Let's go ahead and pray before we get started, and feel free to pray in tongues if you want to."

Well, don't you know...every single one of them started praying in tongues! And yes, it freaked me out. So many things were rushing through my mind. I'd never actually heard people I knew speak in tongues. Deeper than that, though, at a very base level way down within me, my religious alarm bells were going off big-time. Shoot, they were clanging loud enough to wake up the whole apartment complex!

The church I had been raised in didn't even talk about things like this, much less practice them. In fact, I had always questioned whether or not it was even of God. Some Christians I knew thought it wasn't. Yet here I was in what should have been a comfortable Christian setting, and again, just like the revival, I was staring at everyone and feeling out of place. In the middle of a Bible study I agreed with in content, among friends I thought I knew, people I hung out with, and every single one of them... not half of them, or a few of them...every last single one of them was praying in tongues like it was the most natural thing ever.

And it just didn't make sense. I couldn't wrap my head around it or digest it. I didn't focus at all on the study that night, I was too consumed with how in the world every one of these ladies could speak in tongues, and I had no clue. The whole thing sounded so odd, and seemed so fake, that it was very unsettling. I was not willing to be a part of something that might not be truth. Between this and the revival, there were just too many things I wasn't sure about. I had hit a wall.

So I had a decision to make. I loved this group...but I couldn't accept speaking in tongues, and I didn't want to be confronted with it any more. I couldn't even really explain why, other than it scared me because it wasn't how I thought things should be. So in the end, I just didn't go back. I left that session and didn't return, and in a very short time left that church and retreated to the safety of a church more like I was raised in. It offered me all the things I was used to…without making me too uncomfortable.

When I left that group, and that church, and that season of my life, there was one thing I took with me: I had a new clarity for the Bible. I could finally read it and understand it. The prayers over me evidently had great impact, because His Word was opening up and revealing itself to me on a whole new level, and I knew that would never change.

Actually, there were two things I took with me…because I also had the baby in my belly!

CHAPTER 3

YOU HEAR HIM?

"You are probably going to lose this baby."

I had come to this first sonogram with such excitement. I couldn't wait to see that baby and the heartbeat, and indeed I had, but right after the technician pronounced the baby "fine" she had excused herself to go find the doctor. When they came back in I could tell something was not right.

"Your baby is fine, but your cervix isn't," the doctor continued. "It can't handle the weight of the baby, and it is opening. There isn't anything we can do. We could have done a procedure called a cerclage, where we sew the cervix shut, had we known earlier. But I believe we have discovered this too late."

I remember thinking *This can't be happening. This is my miracle baby and I'm not going to let this happen. I can't accept this news.* I told the doctor there had to be a way to do something. I needed a second opinion. In my mind I was thinking *and a third, and a fourth, and a fifth*…whatever it took to make this work.

"I do know a specialist…I have a feeling he will tell you the very same thing, but if you like, I will set you up with him."

I immediately placed all of my hope in this person I had never seen, never met, and didn't know.

"What's his name?" I asked.

"His name is Dr. Angel."

Yep, I thought. *That's my guy. Thank you Lord!*

So we went to see Dr. Angel, and he had a look at my situation. I could tell he was concerned. "This is a hard case," he said, "but we won't give up until we have tried everything possible."

I really liked this guy.

So he gave it a try, and I had surgery the very next day. Wouldn't you know it…it was a success! I now had a cerclage that would save my baby. Dr. Angel was able to make a way where there seemed to be no way, because he was not willing to give up until he had exhausted every possible option. All it cost me was a little faith, and the next seven months on strict bed rest.

And of course, lots of prayer, which usually meant me asking for someone to come by soon so they could get me something and save me from getting up off the couch. The doctor had said I could get up to go to the restroom and to take a shower, but not to get up for anything else if I wanted to keep this baby. And I took him serious.

Through the long seven months we had several challenges with the health of the baby. One sonogram showed that there may be problems around the brain, and the doctors suggested an amniocentesis to rule out anything. But knowing how hard I had worked to get this baby this far, I refused the test because of the increased risk of going into labor. I gave it over to God and the next sonogram came back completely normal.

It's amazing when we take our hands off of things and allow God to do His work. I was beginning to understand I could pray with authority, but I would still follow my prayers with "if it be in your will." Sometimes it was weird, because I would want something so badly, and begin to pray strongly for it, but then immediately feel like I had to add the escape clause: "if it be in your will." If my prayers weren't answered, I could always assume they must not have been in His will. That His plans probably contained a bigger picture I didn't see.

I'm not making fun here, please don't think that. I realize the importance of being in His will, and there is nowhere else I want to be. I don't want to attempt anything or even desire anything if it does not line up with the will of God or my destiny. But when you can't hear God—when the communication is all one way—it is sometimes difficult to know exactly what His will is for a particular situation. If I were to ask should I feed this hungry person, or would it be okay for me to steal this, I know what God's will is for those situations. But what about when I am trying to figure out whether or not we should move to a new house, or take a new job, or which daycare would be best for my child?

So I kept praying in the way I knew, and stayed off my feet while my husband worked and shopped and cooked and went to church and fetched me stuff. The church we had joined was experiencing phenomenal growth. We had attended together for a short time, until I went on what Joe called "couch arrest." After that he continued going on his own.

He joined a Sunday school class, and within a week or two

we found ourselves with an opportunity to buy the house that my husband had grown up in. It seemed like the perfect place to start our new family. It was in the same town, in an area we wanted to be in, with a nice peaceful yard on a lake.

In fact, everything was perfect...except for the fact that my husband was left to pack and move us by himself, because I couldn't do a single thing to help him. So he went to Sunday school class the next week, and stood up in the midst of a bunch of strangers and made the announcement: "I'm moving in two weeks, and I need some help."

One of the couples who came to help was Laurie and Gary, and Laurie and I quickly became friends. A few months later our baby Allie arrived (perfectly healthy, thanks to the Lord and Dr. Angel), and Laurie was the person I called whenever I needed help. For example, it seemed that as perfect as my precious baby was, one day she reached a point where she just would not stop crying. I mean, I swear, I thought I'd broken her! Laurie was the one who came over, and reassured me that no, the kid wasn't damaged...it was probably just gas.

So she and I became real close real fast. She was an only child and I didn't have family in Florida so we became like sisters. We had a great time raising our kids together, loving the Lord, doing Bible studies, all that good stuff. And over time, one of the things I began to notice about Laurie was her super-close relationship with the Lord. It was different than what I was used to. One day we were sitting there talking and she said the Lord had told her something, and I could tell she actually meant...told her something.

I was astonished. "You hear Him?"

"Yes," she said. "Don't you?"

"No...I don't think I do. You mean, actually *hear* Him? You can do that?"

I didn't realize that was even possible for people today. Of course I knew He talked to people in the Bible, and I knew of prophets and others who would say, "God told me such and such," but Laurie was none of these. She wasn't Moses, and she wasn't famous for going around and telling people what new thing God had revealed to her. She was just…Laurie.

I mean, of course I talked to God and asked Him about things, and for things, but I never expected Him to talk back. When I would pray about what to do in a situation, for instance, I would often ask God, but in the end make a decision based on what I believed He would want. I had studied enough about Him and thought I "knew" Him pretty well. I never really put something out there expecting to receive an actual answer.

But oh, man! If this was true, it was a game-changer! If what Laurie was explaining to me was true, and she was actually having real conversations back and forth with God, that was something I had to have! And I had no reason to believe it wasn't true…I mean, it was Laurie!

So from that point on I started trying to hear God's voice. Really hear His voice.

I noticed some things right off the bat, like this thing about ending my prayers with "if it be in your will." I realized that if I actually heard from Him, He could tell me what His will was. I didn't need the disclaimer. So I got up the courage to start asking questions that required a definite yes or no, and expect an answer. I also began to quiet my mind, and focus on listening rather than just talking. Praying no longer meant just throwing something out, but also waiting for something to come back.

This made me realize that so often in the past I would throw out a prayer, and move on without allowing a quiet period to listen. So I began to pause, and develop the patience to wait for an answer. It required an investment of time on my part that hadn't been there before.

And right there, in this newly created time, with this new focus on listening rather than talking, is where it all began to happen. In the quiet time, in the stillness…I began to sense something… like a feeling, or a tug. There was definitely something there.

This was HUGE! This was EXCITING! God, the Creator of the Universe, was communicating to me!

Once I began to feel this, I pressed in even harder. Now that I knew it was real, there was no going back. This wasn't something I was creating, or imagining. It was different than anything I'd ever experienced. It was different than the conversations I had in my head with myself. It was so clearly…not my thoughts. It was something else altogether, and I was certain of it. My dedication and commitment level went through the roof, and the more I pressed in, the deeper I went.

I kept going, and finally felt like I would get a definite sense of *Yes* or *No* when I prayed. I could actually identify it. I would get a peace about a situation, or feel a check in my spirit. Or sometimes I didn't feel anything. I was developing this *yes-no-maybe* relationship with the Lord, which to me was incredibly exciting, because for the first time it meant there was real communication. I knew He heard my prayers, because there was actually something coming back the other direction! Man, I thought I was really rocking!

Until the day Laurie and I were talking, and she shared with me how God had told her to give away her car.

"What…?" I was dumbfounded.

"Yeah," she said, "he told me to give my car to Karen."

"The Lord told you to give your car away...and He actually told you who to give it to? He does that?"

Well, this made it obvious I had a ways to go. I mean, this was such a huge thing. Laurie didn't get new cars every day; actually, she was in the same financial boat I was, and this whole idea just shook my world. Not only had she heard God so specifically, but she was so sure about it—to the point where she was willing to follow through on something so substantial.

It would be one thing for her to believe God told her to give the neighbor twenty dollars, but to be certain that she heard Him say give away her car...that was huge. A huge item which demanded a huge confidence level. And a huge obedience level.

I didn't question whether or not it had been God. I was just shocked. It opened a door for me into a whole new way of thinking—could it really be true that God talked with such specific clarity? And if it was true...oh my goodness, I wanted it! So of course, I started asking lots of questions.

"How do you hear God like that? When did it start? What exactly does He say? What does His voice sound like? Did He say He was going to get you another car? Do you get to pick the color?"

Laurie told me, "Well, I was lying in bed praying, and I heard God say *Car. Karen.* But the understanding I got was I was supposed to give the car to Karen. It was very clear, this knowing I had that filled in the spaces between the words. I questioned Him if what I heard was correct, and He repeated the exact same thing again. *Car. Karen.* And again, just as before, I had the same certainty as to what that meant."

"You mean you actually asked God to repeat Himself? Oh...my...gosh..."

"Yep. So I said, *Okay, God, if this is what you want, then will you make it really, really obvious?* The next day I waited until the evening, when Karen would be home from work, and I called her. We hadn't spoken in months, so I asked her how she was, and she immediately answered that she wasn't so good. It turns out she had been going across the bridge from Tampa to St. Petersburg that very afternoon, (which remember is after God first talked to me) and her car had broken down. She went on to say it was a really old car and had too many problems to fix, so they were going to have to get another one."

"No way!"

Laurie nodded her head. "So I said, that's pretty interesting. Let me tell you what happened...and when I got done telling her what God had said, Karen asked what exactly it all meant."

"It means Laurie's out of a car!" I interrupted. I couldn't believe what I was hearing.

Laurie continued. "I told her I was supposed to give her my car. She asked how much that would cost, but I told her 'no, you don't understand. If He tells me to give it to you, it's yours. We'll get the title transferred, I'll pay for it, and it will be yours.' So that's what we did. And Misty, I'll tell you something else: as soon as I talked to her, I could not get rid of that car fast enough. In my mind, I had somebody else's possession. To the point where I felt guilty even driving it."

I don't know how long it took me to close my mouth. I was obviously amazed that Laurie had given away her only car without thinking about how or where she would get another one. But I was even more amazed that she was so certain... because she heard Him, and she had a definite understanding... she was certain God had told her to do it. This was way beyond *yes-no-maybe.* It hadn't been very long since God revealed to me a whole new level of understanding when it came to reading His Word, but this…this was even bigger!

In fact, this was incredibly eye-opening. Light bulb. Sunrise. This was the beginning of my journey of hearing the Lord, mainly because I trusted Laurie, and I knew her character. I knew what she was saying was true. I had never been around somebody who so matter-of-factly told me "God told me this" or "I heard God say that."

So I became a woman on a mission. I had caught a glimpse of something I was missing, something "more," and I wanted it. As you can imagine, after that I wouldn't stop asking her about it. I had to know…how could I hear God? While I guess I was expecting this really involved super-spiritual answer, this layer-by-layer uncovering of a great lost secret of the ages, what she said kind of took me by surprise…yet sounded vaguely familiar.

"Just pray for it."

"Really?" I said. "That's it? You can do that?"

Oh, man…sometimes I'm such a slow learner. I can personally assure you, from experience, that God is infinitely patient.

So that's what I did. I began to pray to God that I wanted to hear Him like Laurie heard Him, I wanted to communicate with Him in that way. I prayed He would reveal Himself to me, and tell me things in a specific way, where I could be certain it was Him. I don't believe I actually ever asked Him to tell me to give my car away, but I do remember praying like I have never prayed before.

Understand, this wasn't a prayer I offered up once and then stopped. This wasn't a timid prayer, protected by "if it be in your will." This was a whole different kind of prayer for me. This was a serious, ongoing, bold appeal. I knew Laurie had a richness and depth to her relationship with God that I didn't. I was missing something, and I was not going to stop until I had it.

And after many months, I hate to admit, I started to get angry. Ugly questions began to rise up in me, like *What's wrong with me? Why won't God let me have this since I want it so badly? Why does God not love me as much as He loves Laurie?*

I could read His Word now, straight from the Bible. And the Bible was talking to me like never before. I was hearing from God, in the sense I would get a check in my spirit, sometimes... but nothing specific enough and clear enough to make me give away my car, and be so certain about it.

Yes, it was obvious there was more. And since I didn't have it, I did the next best thing: I started relying on Laurie to give me answers from God. What are friends for, anyway? Whenever I came upon a situation and wanted to know what God thought about it (which becomes amazingly common once you know God speaks on things) I would go to Laurie, and I would ask her to ask God. She would, and many times God would have very specific answers for me, through her.

It all seemed to be working pretty well. We were always together. She was my good friend, my trusted prayer partner, my hotline to heaven. But eventually I realized that while this was great, I was stuck. My personal communication with God was not growing, because it didn't need to.

But that was about to change.

CHAPTER 4

DESPERATE

—⁊℘⁊—

By this time Joe and I really wanted another baby, and had been trying inseminations again as regularly as our insurance would allow for the past three years. When all attempts went nowhere, we eventually got set up as foster parents, thinking we would foster to adopt. The whole process took over a year, but we finally got our first child, a little boy named Jonathan. Just as things looked like they were opening up to allow us to move forward with adoption, his mom was released from jail and the judge decided to give her one more chance. I pray it worked out well for them, but of course it was heartbreaking for us.

Right after that we were told about two other children, brothers, who needed a home and were ready for immediate adoption. We had never met them, but when they gave us the information we immediately agreed to take them into our family. There was a court date coming up when the agency would go and present us to the judge as potential new parents, and the lady working the case felt strongly that we would be chosen.

All along the way things looked very much in favor of the boys becoming a permanent part of our family, right up until the final court decision, where they were awarded to another family.

We were crushed. We had prayed about every step, and knew we were being told to move forward through the process. But nothing seemed to have come from it. Our questions for God were many, but they all started with…*Why?*

While we were still tender from this news, and trying to figure all of this out, I got a call about my father. They thought his cancer might have progressed, and they were going to run more tests to find out. My husband was very busy with work at the time, so we decided I would take Allie and go be with my dad.

Off to Tennessee we went, just the two of us.

Well…at least that's what I thought. When Allie and I got to Tennessee, I soon learned there weren't just two of us on the trip…there were three! I was pregnant, again a complete surprise, again by completely natural methods. God had plans to grow our family after all! And, as if that wasn't enough, (since He is the God of more-than-enough) we learned shortly after that the two boys had been adopted by a wonderful couple who were unable to have children of their own.

What a precious time it was to share the news of this pregnancy with my dad in person. There was much celebration in all our lives that day! It was some sweet time with my father. Unfortunately, a few days later the results of the test came back that the cancer had spread. Upon learning this, he gave me a big hug and told me to go back to Florida and "take care of that baby."

Seeing his daughter pregnant brought him such joy, and made me again realize that God's timing is always perfect. I'm forever grateful that he had the opportunity to meet my son Samuel, even though he was in my womb at the time. He was near my father while my father was here on earth, and that has always been special to me.

As soon as I returned home I went immediately to see Dr. Angel. This time we knew what to expect, and I had the cerclage procedure done right away. One great benefit of that was it allowed light bed rest, compared to the strict bed rest of my previous pregnancy. Instead of couch arrest, I guess I was on couch probation. This made the pregnancy much easier, allowing me to travel back and forth to Tennessee and see my dad multiple times before he passed.

When Samuel's birth drew near, my husband and I were so excited. Both of these kids had been a miracle. Our careful planning went right out the window when Samuel decided to come early by about a week, but it still looked like the whole ordeal would go pretty smooth. Unfortunately, that's not exactly how it turned out. During this simple procedure complications arose and I started hemorrhaging. Once the doctors had the baby removed, they had to quickly take the baby and my husband from the room and perform an emergency hysterectomy. It turns out that I had a condition called placenta previa, and had already lost almost three units of blood before they finally got everything under control.

I remember the next morning a few ladies who had been involved in the surgery came into my room to check on me. One of them gave me a lapel pin with a set of angel wings, saying that the angels must have been watching over me because it was a miracle I made it.

I believe the difficulty in recovering from the episode was initially why, when Sam was very young, I began to get the sense that we needed to move back to Tennessee and be around family. Before I was even completely healed, Joe underwent back surgery, and his recovery was also extensive. With Allie now four, and Sam brand-spanking new, it just began to seem like it was time to go "home."

Of course, I didn't realize at the time this was the only way I would ever stop depending on Laurie to hear God for me. Like so much of life, things were happening so fast and tripping all over each other that I wasn't able to get a real clear picture until many years later, when I finally sat down and began to tug at the thread of the amazing journey God had me on. If you would have asked at the time I would have told you it was only because of our growing family. New babies, grandparents, all that.

And I know I prayed about the decision. This was not something that my husband and I would do lightly. We prayed, and I'm sure many times consulted Laurie, and had her pray and ask God on our behalf. And each time, whether it came through what God told her, or it came through me in a sense of peace in my spirit, the answer came back the same...it was time to go.

So we went. My husband sold his company, we left our church, our social group, and our really close friends. We even left our cat, because he was happier at our neighbor's house anyway. He liked to float around in their pool on a float, and we didn't have a pool. (Naturally, we did this with our neighbor's permission.)

And, of course, I left Laurie.

We arrived back in Tennessee in the autumn, right when the leaves began changing. In fact, everything was changing. The big town hustle was replaced by the small town stroll, and life began to come at us with a slower pace, in more manageable bites. It was funny, because when we were in a car and passed someone, they would wave. My husband kept thinking, "Who is that? Do we know them?" It took him a little while to remember that's just what people in the country did: they waved. They were friendly.

What was considered news was changing, too. One morning while I was washing the dishes and listening to the local radio station, they were talking about a man who had called the volunteer rescue squad because his wife had fallen down the hole of the outhouse...and was stuck. No, I'm not lying. They went on to report that after driving around the mountains for almost an hour looking for this man's house, the rescue squad received a call back and he told them never mind, he had pulled her out with the tractor.

If it happened to be a slow news day, you would find front page headlines in the local newspaper about the man who was arrested for stealing power from his neighbor with an extension cord, but there were also big news days like the time the fire department burned down. Other days you just had to shake your head, like when you read that if you came to the flea market at the drive-in movie theater this Saturday, you could actually see...live...Billie Bob the Dancing Goat.

But as exciting as Billie Bob the Dancing Goat was (even live!) Tennessee brought with it a whole new level of alone. I missed my Florida friends.

It started small, the very day we pulled away from Tampa, but this was dismissed as the normal sadness that comes with leaving people you love. Over time, when it should have faded, it didn't. I remember sitting in my house thinking *I should be happy right now, but instead I'm feeling overwhelmed about choices of schools for my daughter, little things about the house, and mainly the fact I can't find a church where we really feel at home.* In Tampa we had lots of friends, church activities, school groups, mom's groups, and so on…all things that took years to establish.

Churches in that area of Tennessee were for the most part very traditional. They were full of love and full of loving people, but the music, the message, and the whole experience of going to church was less free and flowing than what I had come to love in Florida. One thing I associated with the new levels of depth I had been going to with God was the feeling of freedom and openness when it came to worshipping and attending church. I had come to love clapping, and raising my hands during worship, and it just didn't seem like I was going to find that up here.

One of the new places my husband checked out which I didn't attend (sick baby, I believe) was very open, not at all restricted. But after the three hour Sunday service ended up with everyone speaking in tongues, he knew better than to invite me there the following week. However, this didn't change the fact that it was very important to me to find a church to become a member of, to know I was "part of" God's family. It was important to form those friendships, join in those activities…it was important to belong.

And this importance, this need to know the right answer— God's answer—to such a major decision forced me to go to the Lord with a new dedication. I had been pursuing God this whole time, ever since back in Tampa when I knew that there was a level of relationship available I didn't have. I made it a point now to pray about everything. Big things, small things. Which house should we buy, which paper towels should I buy? Seriously…did you ever stand in the store and look at all the paper towels, and wonder, *Okay, this one says it has 1,000 sheets, and this one only has 800, but it says right here that it does a better job with half the sheets, so does that mean…*

I got to the point where I would stop going through all the mental gymnastics in my head (I mean how long can you stand there and study paper towels before people start to say things, especially when you're new in a small town) and I would just pray...*Lord, which paper towels should I buy?*

And believe it or not, many times, I would have a definite peace about a certain one. I don't know that our Father cares that much about what paper towels we use; instead, I choose to believe that He just deeply desires to communicate with us, about anything and everything. He's never too busy to answer the silly questions!

But on this church issue, I was after more than just a sense of peace. I wanted to know. I was after a give-away-your-car type of revelation. I was after clarity and certainty. We had been in Tennessee about six months by this time, and I got desperate. Desperate to know His direction for me. Desperate to know which path was best for my family. Desperate to hear Him.

Please understand, the *yes-no-maybe* guidance that He had been giving me was wonderful, and I was grateful for it. It had served me well when it came to moving my family six hundred miles away, and investing in a home where we could grow and honor Him. I truly believed it even had my family using the best groceries they could have...but when it came to choosing a church, for some reason, I had to hear Him say it.

Well, not exactly "for some reason"...I knew the reason. You see, the church I thought He was going to choose was not necessarily the one I would have picked. And getting this decision right was a little more important than grocery shopping. Standing in the store seeking His direction on paper towels was quite a bit different than deciding on our family's new spiritual home.

Choosing a church...this really mattered. I had to know His will, had to be certain. And that's how I found myself late one night on my knees in the middle of the living room floor. I couldn't sleep because I didn't feel anchored. I needed answers. I TOLD Him (now, please don't take this wrong, but I didn't ASK Him...I was beyond asking.) I TOLD Him: *Father, I MUST hear you. I MUST know exactly which church my family should attend.*

The point is, I was desperate. What a word. What a beautiful, powerful word. My heart, and my soul, and my spirit were desperate, and I cried out to Him, "I have to hear you. I have to know what to do. Father, I must hear your voice!"

And that's when I heard Him say, *East-an-allee.*

Plain as day...I heard Him! Clear as a bell. So clear that if He had told me to give away my car right that second, there's no doubt in my mind I would have done it.

I sat there without moving. I think I was afraid to move because I didn't want the moment to go away. It had really happened! I heard Father God's voice!

I will say that this church was quite different than my church in Florida...I remember in my spirit I was like *YAY!* and then *ohhhhh*, then *YAY!* Either way I was thrilled that I had actually heard Him, because I knew that this was God's best for me and my family. At that point, it was settled. I knew my church, and more importantly, I knew I could hear God's voice.

What I had pursued for so long had just happened! It was a glorious moment. I jumped up from the floor, and danced around the room of my new house. I flew down the hall and back, thinking, *I heard Him! I heard Him!* If everyone hadn't been asleep I would have been screaming at the top of my lungs.

Finally, I just sat down on the couch. And cried happy, happy,

happy tears.

That moment changed everything, because once I knew God could speak to me, actually speak to me, I knew I could expect it in the future. After all these years praying and seeking it, it had finally happened. What an incredible moment. I had discovered that place where I could hear His Spirit speak to my spirit. It was more than a feeling. I was no longer limiting Him to *yes-no-maybe*. I had heard Him speak, as plain and clear as a small-town country morning.

Now, the next Sunday when I went to Eastanallee Baptist Church I cried a little more, right there in the middle of the service. It seemed to be the exact opposite of what I had gotten used to in a church. I mean…it was so traditional. But believe me, there is a huge difference in tears that come from knowing you are where you should be, and tears that come from confusion, from not knowing. I knew this was my church, because I knew this was God's first choice for my family. Those were some sweet tears.

Naturally, the church turned out to be a real blessing. There was so much love there, and so much growth. The pastor and the people were absolutely wonderful, and in a very short time there was no place else I wanted to be. We became their family, and they became ours, and we grew together. In fact, the growth everywhere was incredible. New families continued to join the church because the children's ministry was on fire, and it soon became apparent that an expansion was going to be needed.

Eastanallee was an older church and there simply wasn't enough room. While there was a plan in place to build a new sanctuary on the property, an official vote of the congregation hadn't yet happened. Now, I knew this was important for the church's growth, so I was all in. Joe and I had become well-established by this time, so I joined a group committed to helping the congregation see the dire need for this new building. Our entire goal was to explain exactly what it would mean for the youth and for the future. If you know me, you know: when I say I'm all in, that's not a small deal. My passion, my energy, my not-so-subtle personality, was all focused and on high. Let's just say there wasn't any doubt among the congregation where Misty stood on the issue.

So eventually, I was sitting in the members-only Sunday night service where we were going to vote on the expansion. I was so excited this was finally going to happen. I had a young girl named Stacie sitting beside me. Her mom had been in the hospital with cancer, and the girl had been staying with our family (and taken to calling me Aunt Misty). She was young, and spunky, and full of joy. And at times, I must say, she could be a little bit loud. Anyway, this was an older country church so votes were still tallied by writing on scraps of paper, and the deacons passed them out while the pastor explained one final time what we were voting on. He told us carefully to write only YEA or NAY on the paper, and explained one final time what each vote meant. I was ready.

Now seems like a good time to bring up one thing I had specifically been asking God lately: If I was ever starting to do something that He didn't want me to, please tell me loud and clear.

But even with that being said, I knew without a doubt He wanted this expansion. I had prayed on it many times, and the clarity in His answers had been one of the main reasons I was so passionate about it happening. So there I am, paper in hand, packed in with so many others on the long wooden pews, getting ready to write my long-awaited YEA...when the Holy Spirit intervened.

Write NAY, He said, clearly. Very...very...clearly.

What? I asked. I knew I didn't hear that correctly.

Write NAY.

Oh, man! I just wanted to start rebuking the devil at this point, but there was only one problem...I knew it was my Father's voice. I knew, without a doubt...that's His voice!

Why? I asked.

Silence.

This didn't make sense. *Talk to me, God, please. Why?*

More silence.

Panic began to set in. *I can't do that God! What will people think if they see this? They'll think I'm a hypocrite! I'm not a hypocrite, God! You know I'm not a hypocrite! Why are you doing this to me?*

So many emotions, fears, confusion in that brief three minute time slot. But reluctantly, and silently, covering it with my hand, I finally wrote down NAY.

As soon as I did it, I felt a great release, but I still didn't understand it. I folded the paper and gave it to the young girl next to me so she could pass it down to the waiting man at the end of the pew. Of course instead of passing it, she took a peek... and saw what I wrote.

Did I mention she wasn't always the most quiet little girl?

"AUNT MISTY!" she said, "YOU WROTE NAY! Why? What

are you doing?"

I wanted to melt. "Shh, Stacie!" I said. "We'll talk later."

"But why would you do that?" Her sweet little voice continued to get louder. "You want the expansion!"

Yes, I wanted the expansion, but right now I also wanted to run out of the room. I know my face was ten shades of red. I didn't turn to look at anyone.

"But the pastor said NAY means NO, that you don't want…"

It only took me half an hour to get her to finally quiet down. At least it seemed that way. Let's just say by the time she finally passed the paper there were no more secrets in God's house about the way Aunt Misty voted. My eyes stayed fixed forward at the man behind the podium for the rest of the service. At the end of what seemed like an eternity, a deacon came up to read the results of the vote.

"The vote was Yea 87, Nay 4."

I'm not sure if anyone looked at me or not, because I made it a point not to look at them. But if they did, they saw me smiling, because I was so happy. And relieved. We had done it! The church would get the new building. Evidently we had done a great job of rallying everyone to vote for it, because I was one of only four that voted against it! Oh, you know God and I definitely had a conversation coming…

I didn't wait until I got home to go into some serious "prayer" time, I got after it as soon as I hit the car. I felt like an angry Mom sitting God down in the corner.

God, I really need you to explain!

And sure enough, He answered right away…and His voice

was so gentle, so sweet. *Misty, you got what you wanted. The expansion happened, and you were an important part of that. But what I wanted from you today was obedience, even in things you don't understand. I am so proud of you..."*

Oh, my heart melted and my tears began to flow. I had been faithful and obeyed. Even when it was uncomfortable and didn't make sense. God was proud of me!

That moment changed my life and I was able to go to Stacie and explain to her why I had voted that way. I was able to share it in my Bible study class at the church, and it was a lesson that was written on my heart for the many more times of obedience that would be needed in the future.

Obedience is better than understanding.

But the fact remains I would not have chosen that little country church on my own. And look what all I would have missed. It took hearing my Father, actually hearing Him say, *This is my best for you,* to open up a rich new depth to our relationship.

And that took me getting desperate. I truly believe that was the key. Earlier I had wanted it, really desired it. But I wasn't desperate. When I reached a point where I had to know what God said, and nothing else mattered...my thoughts on the churches, which worship or preaching style I preferred, the scenarios I played out about what it would be like to attend there, the whole checklist of pluses and minuses, and even the *yes-no-maybe* I relied on to choose paper towels...when all these things didn't matter, and the only thing that mattered was hearing God's voice, God's voice was exactly what I heard.

Looking back on that season, this was when I learned that home is where God is. It's not about your friends, your family, or even your church...home is where God is, and church is where God is. In Florida, I had always been searching for the feeling of home, and I thought if I moved back to Tennessee I would be home. And in Tennessee I had been searching for what I considered the perfect church. But moving into this new level of closeness with God made me realize where I was, physically, wasn't what mattered, because life is seasonal, and seasons will change.

I am home when I get to a point in my life where I am walking side-by-side with God, and I get my foundation from Him, and I get my guidance, love, and joy from Him. Then home is wherever He puts me, and home is wherever He has me. And I am in church…well, always.

Church was never meant to be a particular building. God's church were the people who followed Jesus, and they were sent into the world, and the countryside, and their own neighborhood to love people and reveal God's Truth to them. Church is where God is, and God is everywhere. His congregation is the world, and His ministry is everyone, and church is always in session. We should walk, and talk, and love, and worship, and yes, speak to God, all day long and wherever we happen to be.

My relationship with God during this season continued to grow stronger and stronger. Hearing from Him was not an immediate thing that one day was not there and then came in a flood. But once I knew it was available to me, I would seek it and wait for it. And you would be surprised what we talked about. It turns out He's got a few things on His mind, too…and He loves to share them.

But even though all these incredible things were going on, I still really missed Florida. I missed my friends. While I was in Tennessee, my Florida friends would come stay with me a few weeks at a time, and then I would go stay with them a few weeks. This went on for the several years we were living there. The experience of moving to Tennessee spurred such good growth in me, because I was forced to stop depending on Laurie to hear God for me. You might say, I got desperate enough to put everything else in my life way back in second place. Hearing His voice, clearly, confidently, was the only thing that mattered.

And once that was settled, He told me, *You can go back to Florida now.*

CHAPTER 5

BIG & MORE

When I came back to Florida, I didn't have any doubts about whether or not it was the right move, because God was coming with me. One thing Tennessee developed in me was a desire for small town living. Our town had been tiny, just a single exit off the interstate. It was the kind of place where you get off the interstate and follow the arrow, pass a couple flashing lights and think...*Was that it?*

So we settled into a smaller area south of Tampa, around Sarasota, and joined a local church we really clicked with. It seemed like they were overflowing in love and had that familiar structure I wanted for the kids. I began getting engrossed in Bible studies and got to know a bunch of super people. One of these was a Bible teacher named Dee, who became a real spiritual mentor for me. She was full of wisdom, and I admired that and wanted to learn all I could from her. One study we went through was <u>Discerning the Voice of God</u> by Priscilla Shirer. If you have not done it, I highly recommend it.

While I was already hearing God speak to me, and could definitely discern that it was His voice, this study took me deeper in a number of ways. It highlighted listening more actively, more purposefully...setting aside time to shut everything else out, invite the Holy Spirit to speak into my life, and to listen with anticipation. This was huge, because while I had thought I already had been setting aside "God time," once I really became purposeful about it I realized there was so much more I could do. For instance, I used to wake up at 3am in the morning and roll over and go back to sleep. Now I began to realize that many times when I woke up that early it was because the Father had something to say, and I would grab my Bible and head to my favorite chair and say, *Okay, God...here I am.*

My personal time with God soon became more fruitful than my time in church. I kept going to church and gathering together with other Christian friends, but I purposely grew the time I spent with God, alone. I reprioritized other things that were filling my life and replaced them with God time. I never felt shorted or cheated...quite the opposite, I felt richer and fuller and more satisfied than ever. It was mind-blowing to think that I could actually spend real "alone time" with the Creator of the Universe...just the two of us, hanging out and talking.

The voice of God reveals His character. The more time I spent listening to the Father, the more I felt captured by His love. A love that was powerful enough to create the world, and a love that was pure enough to redeem it. Sometimes this love would pour over me, and lay on me like a thick blanket, and there were simply no words to describe the sensation. I can tell you this: nothing was missing!

While I was always excited to rest and spend time with God, I also became eager to go and do whatever He would place on my heart; eager to obey His words. Not only because my love was so great, but also because of the fruit I would see come from it.

I committed during this time to be completely obedient...to go and do and say whatever He revealed to me, without hesitation or second thoughts. And with no whining!

And...this is a big one...no matter how ridiculous it seemed.

During this time God was lovingly growing my faith, and opening up the understanding that His way of dealing with situations was not the world's way. While His responses were always completely based in love, and completely based in truth (because He is Love and Truth) sometimes they still didn't make a whole lot of sense. They were far from "normal."

But that was okay. I was getting to a place in my heart where I was willing to look foolish for God. Discerning and obeying His voice was not only the highest form of praise I could offer, but also the greatest form of blessing I could receive. So I made it a point to capture every word. I expected they would come, and when they did I made certain that none of them fell away empty.

I was completely surrendered. Completely sold out. I mean, come on, I was talking to God! Having conversations that were as real as any conversation I would have with anyone else! To be here, after so many years of feeling like I was missing something, of knowing there was more but not knowing what it was, how could I not be?

I could hear Him very specifically now, and was chasing Him with everything I had. I was digging into my Bible to the point where I couldn't get enough of it. My appetite for God and anything He had to say was insatiable. I would regularly wake up two hours early just to have time alone with Him before anyone else got up. That time of undivided attention with God was so important to me.

And the beautiful thing was, the more I read my Bible, the more I talked with Him, the more I sat and listened for Him, the more I sought Him every day, the more relationship we had. The better friends we became. It was incredible. There was a part of me being uncovered and being nourished by Him I had not even known was hidden. And there were also parts of Him being uncovered, constantly. There was always something new and fresh and surprising, like discovering His incredible sense of humor.

He's not only fun, He's also funnier than anyone I know, because His humor is always unexpected. It would come at the most surprising times. I'd be talking to Him about something serious, and He would come back with this one-liner and just crack me up! I can't count the times during prayer I just busted out laughing, saying, *God, you are so funny!*

Humor is one of the most direct pathways to joy, and the Father is all about joy!

The more He showed me, the more I knew I needed. The more I discovered, the more I knew He had for me. The closer we became, the more aware I was of the distance still between us. Not in a bad way, in a good way. It didn't feel like He was convicting me for the space that still remained; it felt more like He was an excited kid who couldn't wait to show me the things He had yet to reveal. I knew, in my spirit, that He was as thrilled and eager and excited for this level of relationship as I was. We were like two kids having fun together exploring a new forest.

Along about this time He began to tell me, every time we sat down, that something big was about to happen. He kept coming back to it, and emphasizing that it was big…every time I thought I had my mind wrapped around big, He would say, *Misty…BIG*, and take it to a whole new level. This was God-sized. It was exciting, and a little scary, although that's not the right word because there was no fear associated with it. The Bible speaks of the fear of the Lord, but it's not fear as in being scared. It's a level of awe, of wonder, that causes an exhilaration unlike anything you've ever known.

And then one day…he gave me a verse. He was always leading me to things in His Word, revealing things that fit the situation or answered a question in my head. But this was different. He revealed to me a verse that was so powerful, it set the entire direction of my new walk with Him:

Forget the former things; do not dwell on the past. See, I am doing a new thing! Now it springs up; do you not perceive it? I am making a way in the wilderness and streams in the wasteland.

Isaiah 43:18-19 NIV

I knew immediately this was what He had been talking about. This was the "BIG." I mean it's not like it was very hard to discern. God said, *Misty, this is BIG.*

He told me He was putting me into a new ministry, and that He was preparing me. He didn't give me details, and I knew there was more hidden than revealed. He's a smart God, and He had seen me run away before when too much was revealed at once. This time He took it a little slower...

Look, He said. *I am showing you a new way. It's going to be like nothing you have ever known.*

I was thinking, *Am I going to move?*

Misty, it's going to be like nothing you have ever known...

Am I going to a new church, Father?

There will be rivers in the desert.

Okay! Rivers in the desert...Living Waters...but what's dry?

God, I feel more drenched in your love right now than I ever have!

You are going to have a new ministry.

Oh, man! A new ministry! Show me, Father, show me! I'm ready…

But He didn't show me. Not that day, not that week. In fact, this preparation went on for almost six months. Every day He would talk about it, but every day didn't bring new information. He spoke the same message: He was preparing me. He was making me ready. He was bringing something big, something life-changing, and I knew it was so, because I knew Him. And because He knew me, He was revealing it to me in the most sensitive, most loving way possible. He didn't dump it on me… he was taking great care to make sure I was ready.

But when it came, I'm still not sure I was…

A group of us ladies from the Bible study would gather together at Dee's house regularly, just to get together and pray for each other and whatever else needed praying about. One day we were there, gathered around the coffee table, praying for another lady that was there. She had been raised in a different religion, one that had involved a lot of idol worship, and fortune telling, and the like.

I remember we were in a circle, and Dee was praying out loud, and we were praying for this other girl. That was the whole point, was to pray for this other girl. I'm stressing that because of what happened next.

As we prayed through different things she had been involved in, I was becoming convicted of the fact that I, too, had engaged in fortune telling in the past. I had played with fortune-telling cards, and had gone as far as going to a fortune teller for fun. I even remember my friends and I playing with the Ouija board when I was a little girl. Not to mention, one time a bunch of us young girls (from the church youth group, no less) got together at a sleepover and had a séance. What sense does that make?

These childhood memories kept coming up while we were praying for this other lady, and in my heart I began to repent of all these occurrences in my life. All of a sudden my chest had this incredible pressure on it and I felt a horrible tightening in my throat, like a choking feeling. It was every bit as serious as if someone was right behind me, squeezing my throat and chest. It could not be correctly described as uncomfortable, or annoying, or even scary. It was terrifying.

And then I felt—didn't imagine, but actually felt—something release and lift off of my body.

As crazy as it was, it could not be ignored. And it could not be denied. It wasn't something we could come back to later, after we were done with the other girl. I mean, my issue was all of a sudden demanding center stage, and as awkward as it was, I couldn't do anything about it!

"Girls!" I screamed, interrupting them in the middle of their prayer for this other lady, "I have to stop you! I mean, y'all need to pray for me, RIGHT NOW!"

I had my hands on my chest, and I'm sure I had a pretty crazy look on my face. "You don't understand…something just got up off of me and left! I mean, like it was ON me and I just felt it get up and leave!"

Can you imagine?

Never before in my life would I have dreamed of breaking into a prayer circle and saying, "Oooh—stop praying for her! Right now! Everybody pray for me instead!" I mean, how stinking rude is that? But I'm telling you, I had no choice. This was not a normal feeling or strong emotion...this was something that had been sitting on me, that I didn't even know was there, and I had just felt it physically lift off of me. And God bless Dee. She just turned her attention from the other girl and directed it toward me and kept right on praying.

After all the others had left, I was talking to her about it. "What was that? It was bizarre!"

"Well," she said, "I don't know a lot about it, but it sounds like deliverance."

"Deliverance? What's deliverance?"

"It's where something..."

She seemed to search for a better word, but evidently didn't find one. "Demons...are on you, and they get...cast off. Get up and leave."

Whoa.

This was a new thing for me. I didn't know anything about demons, and wasn't sure where I stood on the subject as a Christian. I mean, of course I knew they were bad. I knew they were evil, definitely on the "other team." Not on God's team. But what exactly were they? Could a Christian have a demon? Were they in people, on people? Wasn't all that stuff only in the Old Testament? How did a demon and the Holy Spirit reside in the same person, since light and darkness cannot co-exist? So many questions, so many things I was not clear about, but one thing was for sure: something was sitting on me and I FELT IT GET UP AND LEAVE.

"I have a friend in another state who is in a deliverance ministry," Dee continued. "Let's call her and talk to her—she can explain more about it."

So we called her friend and she confirmed, yep, that sounded just like a demon. She said it matter-of-factly, but to me, I was... well...creeped out at the thought of it. That it was in me. Or rather, on me. Or whatever.

She went on to tell us that a demon spirit can oppress (not possess) a Christian, and that many times they come by our invitation, when we engage in things such as fortune telling. She recommended a book I should read, Deliver Us from Evil, by Don Basham. It turned out that Dee had one at her house (a copy of the book, not a demon) that her friend had given her fifteen years earlier.

When I read through the book I was amazed at the similarities between what the author had experienced and the events, feelings, and emotions I went through. There was difficulty breathing, and a strong sense of something on me, physically, and when it left not only was I stunned but there was also a definite sense of feeling lighter. I could tell that it was no longer there.

So what started out as a day going to pray for someone else ended up with me being delivered. This opened up a whole new aspect of the spiritual battle we face. After that day I gained a new understanding of this passage:

For our struggle is not against flesh and blood, but against the rulers, against the authorities, against the powers of this dark world and against the spiritual forces of evil in the heavenly realms.

Ephesians 6:12 NIV

Well, God was right...this was BIG.

And as you can imagine, I had so much to talk to Him about! There's no better feeling than to know that you can bring up a subject to God and discuss it with Him as easily as you would talk back and forth to a good friend. My eyes were opening to a whole new reality, or rather a new understanding of reality.

I guess I had known that demons were real, that there was a battle going on between light and darkness...that's basic Bible 101. But reading it in the Bible was way different than having it happen in real life. To realize I had been walking around with one, for a very long time, was mind-boggling! I mean, I hadn't engaged in fortune telling since I was young, but there was no doubt I walked in with that thing on me, and I left without it! Who knew that could happen?

I have run into Christians since who I relate this story to, and some of them have a hard time with it. They want to get down in the details and debate, and quote scripture about this, that, or the other. But there is no debate in my mind whether or not a Christian can be oppressed by a demon. I do know a Christian can't be "possessed" since we as Christians belong to God, however, we can be oppressed, which is essentially us giving demons the authority to harass us.

But either way, as for the questions of whether or not they are real, and whether or not they can cause Christians great trouble, and whether or not through the authority of the Holy Spirit we can make them leave through repentance and deliverance, for me that's been settled. I've now seen it too many times, and in my mind there's no argument.

When I was younger, somehow I got the sense that once I was saved everything in my life was supposed to be wonderful. To the point that when I did hit rough times, it made me question whether I was truly saved or not. I would wonder what I was doing wrong, and why God was mad at me. Or worse yet, I didn't wonder, because I thought I knew. In any case, it led to a lot of needless guilt, and caused me to focus on my works rather than on His love and grace.

Once I seriously began to engage in the battles going on in the spiritual realm, kingdom battles between light and dark, I finally realized that getting saved basically draws the enemy's attention. Before you are saved the enemy doesn't care about you too much, because he's not having to worry about you bringing new people into the Kingdom. But as a Christian, especially one who is engaged in the battle, the last thing he wants is for you to be successful. So you will begin to get attacked more, and the more effective you are at winning souls to Jesus, the stronger the attacks get.

But...and here's the good part...the devil never wins. After a while, we start realizing His ways and know when it's him. We start turning those situations around to show God's glory, and with this comes a peace beyond understanding, joy like you've never known, and an ability to love to a degree you never thought possible. The wonderful mysteries of the Kingdom begin to unveil before you, and the more engaged in the battle you become the more of these beautiful blessings become available. The presence of God, the power of the Holy Spirit, the authority and power of Love, and Light, and Truth...all of these become increasingly available as you become more and more engaged.

The enemy is not your friend. He's going to do whatever he can to trip you up. A lot of Christians say, "I don't know why God is doing this to me" when something bad happens. Many times we bring consequences on ourselves by our bad choices, and we want to blame God for it. I had played these stupid little fortune telling games innocently. Never did I suspect that I was opening a door to allow a demon to oppress me. But now I know that sometimes our own actions can invite these problems into our life.

So you're not imagining things. The enemy is coming after you, and he's probably trying to hit you where you're most vulnerable. But God is aware of this, and if you allow Him to, He will turn these evil ploys around and use them for something good. God does not create your bad circumstances, but He also won't miss the chance to bring beauty from the ashes. Instead of blaming God, or avoiding God, run to Him! Go to Him immediately, and ask Him, *What are we gonna do about this?*

I promise you, God will show you how to shut the enemy up. He will cause your enemy, and his evil little demons, to flee. Up against God's authority, they have no power. When Light comes in, darkness has to flee.

Our Heavenly Father is truly amazing. I love how, time and time again, He has lovingly prepared me for what He is going to ask me to do next. He loves me huge, but because He knows me intimately He loves me in tiny steps. And it could have stopped right there, with getting free of this demon at Dee's house. If God had just wanted to deal with this ugliness in my life simply to bless me, I would have been eternally grateful.

But as BIG as this was, there was MORE. These two words have come to describe my walk with God. If you get anything out of this book, let it be that God operates in the realm of BIG and MORE.

CHAPTER 6

IT'S REAL!

It was summer, and the ladies and I took a break from our regular Bible study. The group decided it would be a good idea to get together a couple of times and have a book swap. We were all reading different books outside of the current study, and this would be an opportunity to share the ones that had really moved us.

Chloe, one of the ladies in the Bible study, gave me a book by Andrew Wommack entitled Spirit, Soul, & Body. Sitting in the big living room chair curled up with the book, I knew something was up. My first hint was the highlighter. I eventually just put it down, because I realized that pretty much every word on every page was getting yellowed. I was definitely going to need to buy Chloe another book. But more than that, it was the Holy Spirit within me, jumping with excitement. It felt like my chest was popping like popcorn! I just kept hearing from God, *There is truth here! There is truth here!*

I was certain this was a bigger part of the picture of what God had been talking about. God had not stopped telling me that there was something more coming, something BIG. He kept repeating the verse that He had shown me, highlighting it in the craziest ways.

There were new rivers springing up; He was doing a new thing…

And I knew, without a doubt, that this book was exactly where God wanted me, and that it had something to do with my new ministry. This was what the many months of preparation had been leading to. Everything that was being revealed in these pages was like a long-searched for puzzle piece that fit perfectly into some empty, open place in my spirit which I hadn't even known existed. I don't mean empty in a negative way. During this time my spirit was more full than it had ever been. I mean empty in the sense that it was prepared, it was ready to receive. I was ready to receive.

Chapter after chapter I was like *Yes! Yes! Yes!*

And all along the way God was cheering me on. *Go! Go! Go!*

This incredible book said when you are saved, your spirit is the part of you that is completely changed. Your old human spirit is replaced by God's Spirit, living in you. Old things pass away. All things become new.

Forget the former things…do not dwell on the past…I am doing a new thing!

It explained to me that this new Spirit, when placed in us, was lacking nothing. It was complete, and completely God! Spiritual-mindedness, focusing on things of the Spirit, would release the flow of God's Holy Spirit into our soul, while carnal-mindedness, or focusing on things of the world, would stop the flow. But the

Spirit was ready...it was all there, within us, completely God, from the day we first got saved. We just had to discover how to get it to flow into the dry places within our soul.

I am creating rivers in the desert...

I was so excited, I just knew this was what God had for me; I could sense the rivers beginning to flow across the dry desert. I kept reading at a furious pace, chapter after chapter. I was devouring every word, because I knew it was true. Finally, I flipped the page and started reading about...speaking in tongues.

Crud, I thought. *This book seemed so good. I wish he hadn't gone there...*

And I actually closed the book...and put it down.

It's difficult to explain, but as much as the Holy Spirit in me was confirming that what I was reading was truth, speaking in tongues was simply somewhere that my mind and my emotions couldn't go. I had built up a wall against "tongues," and it was tall and it was strong. The whole thing seemed weird, and fake, and made me very uncomfortable. I thought that speaking in tongues was not of God, even though I wasn't sure why.

But as soon as the book hit the coffee table, I heard God say, *Stop. Pick it back up. Just because it makes you uncomfortable doesn't mean it's not true. This book is truth, and you need to read it as truth.*

Wow. I had to take a couple minutes thinking about that one. Just because something makes me uncomfortable doesn't mean it's not true.

Interestingly enough, the book had told me (and I probably even highlighted!) that my feelings should actually be the caboose, not the engine. My feelings were designed by God to follow what I knew to be true, not to lead the way. This book explained that if I continued to let the caboose act like the engine in my life, I would find myself either going nowhere or heading straight for a train wreck!

Boy, God was ready for me this time. He had me covered from every angle.

So I picked the book back up, and I continued reading, thinking—no, knowing—that God was in it. It took away any ability I had to read it and doubt, because God had told me to finish it, and that it was truth. I had clearly heard Him say it. So I began to read again, without my guard up. I didn't need to protect myself from a lie, because He already told me it was truth. I was able to take what I knew—or thought I knew—and set it aside, and simply have faith in what I was yet to learn.

Much like I had been practicing with obedience, and following His voice without question, there was now no question I was going to finish this book.

Toward the end it began talking about the baptism of the Holy Spirit, which was a phrase I didn't fully or completely understand. In the past it had been one of those things that confused me, because the word baptism had a very specific meaning to me. I was only aware of one baptism, with water, and I had already done that. Nevertheless, here it was, so I read on and tried to grasp what it had to say. There was a prayer to receive the baptism of the Holy Spirit, so with an open mind, and belief in my heart, I prayed the prayer.

And nothing happened.

I knew I had prayed it with the right heart, truly open and desiring it. For good measure I also prayed, *Father, I desire to speak in tongues.*

And nothing happened.

The next day I got up, curious to see if anything would happen since I had prayed the baptism prayer the night prior. Still nothing. I had my regular time with the Lord and to be honest, I'm not sure if I was relieved or disappointed that nothing had happened. I was sort of on the fence.

Well, the following day I came off the fence. In fact I jumped off the fence. I had a new attitude...I had to know! I started praying again. Praying in earnest. Praying serious. Praying forcefully. There was something here God wanted me to have, and I wasn't getting it. I finally put the Bible down and, out loud, said, "God, I want what you have for me! I have to know truth!"

Oooh, do you see what happened there? Did you catch that? I was getting desperate again!

Boy, I have such a great respect for desperation. I truly believe it's a powerful, powerful place to be. And from that place in my Spirit, from that point of desperation, I cried out, "Father, I have to know truth! I cannot live another day without knowing the truth! Is healing of today? Is the baptism of the Holy Spirit of you? Is speaking in tongues of you? Father, I can't take another breath without knowing truth!"

And sitting there, on my tattered couch in my little house, this...yummy-yummy warmth, like a fire...began to grow in my belly. It continued to rise up into my chest, neck, and then throat. I just knew to open my mouth and when I did I started speaking this most wonderful, ridiculous, beautiful language that made no sense...but it made perfect sense. It was heaven, flowing through my vocal cords. It was life, and love, and truth, and joy...

For the first time I really understood the term "caught up in the Spirit." I felt like I was floating, soaring! Rivers of blessing came flooding through my dry body. This was so definitely a new thing! And it went on and on and on. I remember thinking, like a little excited girl, *I'm speaking in tongues! I'm speaking in tongues!*

Never before had anything felt this good. It was crazy good! It was incredible! This must be what heaven feels like! I'm sitting here trying to write this and capture the moment right now. Any words I think of just seem to fall short...I can tell you this: it was exciting. And scary, but a good scary. Rivers of Living Water were flowing and filling me. Filling my dry places. Filling the entire room, my entire world.

Forget the former things; do not dwell on the past. See, I am doing a new thing! Now it springs up; do you not perceive it? I am making a way in the wilderness and streams in the wasteland.

I felt the Lord's presence directly. It was so powerful that my hands were shaking. Close is not even the right word; it was beyond close. The Holy Spirit of God, which is Love, and His Holy Spirit in me were one and the same and in perfect harmony. I was complete. And full of Life! I have never, even to this day, felt such a pure love. It is indescribable, other than to say it is the very meaning of life. The reason we live.

There was a clarity, a boldness that came on, and I knew that I knew that I knew that this was all real and no one could ever tell me different. All doubt was gone. All confusion was gone. All the walls were torn down. I felt God taking me up to the top of the mountain. I didn't know exactly what it meant at the time but I knew it was something good.

When the experience was over, my family was still sleeping, because I had gotten up early to pray. I went running into the bedroom and jumped on the bed to wake my husband. I'm sure

I shocked him silly but all I could say was "It's real! It's real! Healing is of today, speaking of tongues is of God...Joe, it's all real!"

That day when I walked outside the grass was greener. I'm not kidding, everything was crisper and sharper. It was like God was using a new kind of paint to color the world. The trees were more alive. The birds were singing louder. The very air was different...the way I took it into my body was no longer the same. It was His breath, entering my body...the very breath of life! This was BIG!

Breathe Freedom Ministries had been born.

As the days went by, I was like a child in a new land. I was experiencing something I had never imagined. It was almost like I was awakened to a hidden world. It took a few days, then my tongues came again during prayer. Shortly after that, I was walking in the back yard and started singing in tongues! This was just incredible. I didn't know who to talk to about all this, so I called Andrew Wommack's prayer line. I remember saying something like, "I had this incredible experience I can't even describe, then I started speaking in unknown tongues. I don't have any close friends that speak in tongues, so what do I do?"

(I didn't mention I had run away from all my tongue-speaking friends long ago...)

The sweet lady on the phone was so patient. I'm sure she had experienced this many times. She told me just to speak in tongues each day, that it was my spirit praying to God. The Holy

Spirit in me knew exactly what to say and what I needed, so just let it flow. She suggested when I was driving in my car, speak in tongues. When I was washing the dishes, pray in tongues. It would bring in God's presence and help align me with God. I remember thinking, *Why doesn't everyone know about this? Why wouldn't everyone do this?*

But then I remembered how hard I ran from it, every time God tried to reveal it...

After the first week, I got up the courage to call Dee and tell her what was going on. I would have called Laurie too but she was gone on a six week vacation up north, in a cabin, and it was hard for her to get reception on the cell phone at times. I wasn't sure what Dee would think of all this. We had just never talked about...this topic before. To me this was even bigger than "demons."

Nevertheless, I took a deep breath and jumped in: "Here's what's going on," I told her over the phone. "You know God has been telling me that something new and BIG was coming, and, well..."

I could tell she was listening close, trying to digest every word.

"I read this book that talked about the baptism of the Holy Spirit..."

I paused briefly to give her a chance to jump in, but of course she didn't.

"And it had this prayer, and I said this prayer, and I had...the most incredible experience..."

The line was still silent.

"And I started...speaking in tongues...What do you think

about that?"

"Oh, Misty," she said softly. "I speak in tongues, too."

Oh man...I was floored! I had gone to church with her, done Bible studies with her, counseled with her for years. She was a spiritual mentor, for crying out loud! I had no clue! We went on talking about tongues and the baptism of the Holy Spirit and she let me know that, yep, she was right there with all of it. Had been for a long time, in fact.

"Dee," I said, finally, "Why didn't you tell me about this?"

Her answer landed like a punch in my heart: "Well...a lot of people in our church speak in tongues...it's just not something we talk about...openly."

I could actually feel the Holy Spirit inside of me grieving. I felt His warm tears filling my insides, and breaking through my eyes.

This made absolutely no sense. The richness and depth of my relationship with God had gone from 10 to 10,000. Why would any church not talk about this? Why would this not be lesson number one in every New Believers class?

And then it came to me. I recalled my previous church, where I had encountered the love and freedom of the Holy Spirit for the first time. The one where I first got a glimpse of the Holy Spirit's power, when I became pregnant after the laying on of hands. I had been so in love with the freedom of this new aspect of God, and so thankful that He was finally revealing the "more" I knew I had been missing, and so confident that He had worked a miracle in my belly through my new friends. But even with so much confirmation every day that my relationship with God was growing to a point I had never thought possible, I had to walk away when I hit what I considered to be a non-negotiable.

As soon as I was confronted with speaking in tongues, I was gone.

So it seems many churches have made a choice: since the main thing they want to do is introduce people to Jesus and get them saved, and since the last thing they want to do is run people off, they concentrate mainly on the salvation message. Their focus and their teachings lean heavily toward the Father and the Son, but don't really dig too deeply into the Holy Spirit.

This is how I had come to love the Father, and love Jesus Christ, and love my salvation, but not really know the Holy Spirit. This is how my idea of "growing my relationship with God" had come to mean reading more, studying more, and concentrating on getting better at abiding by the list of do's and don'ts. I had no idea for many years that the do's and don'ts would work themselves out so long as I concentrated on growing the personal relationship in the way God had originally intended, through the Holy Spirit.

This is how I had ended up to be a Christian who still felt something was missing. Since I hadn't been taught that speaking in tongues was of God, it made me feel like it was weird. God is not weird. The Father is not weird, the Son is not weird, and the Holy Spirit is not weird. While it is true that He doesn't confine Himself to natural laws—the things of God are foolishness to the world, and the things of the world are foolishness to God—it doesn't mean that He is weird. As a point of clarification, people are sometimes weird, but if that's the case they would be weird with or without the baptism of the Holy Spirit.

But that didn't change the fact that growing up, my particular church was very much in favor of the baptism of water (as taught in the Bible) but they didn't teach the baptism of fire and the Holy Spirit (as also taught in the Bible). And now, I felt like when it came to my relationship with God, I had discovered this whole new hidden treasure. Like all along I had this shiny set of keys, which was my salvation...but I had just discovered the car that's been sitting in the garage this whole time!

Salvation had been firmly settled in my mind. I loved Jesus Christ, and believed I had eternal life. I was a Christian and I knew it. I had discovered Love, and Truth, and had found the Way. I had fallen in love with His church, and become deeply involved, leading Bible studies and serving specific ministries. I was able to give a good explanation of my faith, and had led many others to love and accept Jesus Christ as their Lord and Savior.

But for the longest time I just didn't understand that there was...more.

Not more to salvation; Jesus is all you need. Not more to calling yourself a Christian; Jesus is all you need. Not more that is necessary for God to see you as without sin; Jesus is all you need. And certainly not more to get to heaven. Jesus is all you need!

But I don't know how many times I read where John the Baptist said:

I baptize you with water, for repentance. But after me comes one who is more powerful than I, whose sandals I am not worthy to carry. He will baptize you with the Holy Spirit and fire.

Matt 3:11 NIV

I mean if I really wanted to understand baptism, shouldn't I listen to John the Baptist? But I don't know why it didn't click when I read:

Suddenly a sound like the blowing of a violent wind came from heaven and filled the whole house where they were sitting. They saw what seemed to be tongues of fire that separated and came to rest on each of them. All of them were filled with the Holy Spirit and began to speak in other tongues as the Spirit enabled them.

Acts 2:2-4 NIV

And if perhaps I thought that this second baptism was only for the original Apostles, the Bible told me that Paul said to the new disciples:

'Did you receive the Holy Spirit when you believed?' They answered, 'No, we have not even heard that there is a Holy Spirit'…when Paul placed his hands on them, the Holy Spirit came on them, and they spoke in tongues and prophesied.

Acts 19:2,6 NIV

The new believers had not even heard. Think about that a moment…they had not even heard that there was a Holy Spirit.

CHAPTER 7

PRAY FOR CHLOE

———— ❧ ————

Within a couple weeks of all this, God asked me to pray for someone.

It happened like this: Bible study was starting back up and I was substitute-teaching for Dee that day, as she had to be elsewhere and couldn't lead the class. As it was wrapping up for the day, God told me I needed to pray for Chloe, the lady who shared the Andrew Wommack book with me. He didn't give me any more information, so it felt a little awkward to walk up to her out of the blue. But again, I was focusing on doing whatever I heard God say, whenever I heard Him say it.

This particular time, I just knew…or more correctly my spirit knew. One thing I think people struggle with is they somehow think it's less real if you don't audibly hear a voice, but that's not so. The Spirit of God resides in us, and will speak to us in Spirit and in Truth. It won't always be heard in the physical realm, but that doesn't make it any less real. It's communication from Spirit to spirit, not necessarily a sound that passes from mouth to ear.

Remember, the physical realm is the smallest part of what's actually going on. There is an entire spiritual realm that is not limited by time, space, or distance. Things like gravity, sound, and growing old have no relevance there. But the Bible tells us this realm is real, and it tells us this is where the real action takes place. For our struggle is not against flesh and blood (the physical realm) but against the rulers, against the authorities, against the powers of this dark world and against the spiritual forces of evil in the heavenly realms. As Christians, if we limit our understanding to what we can see, feel, touch, hear, and taste...we're missing the largest part of the battle—and the largest part of the blessing.

So, anyway, God said, *You need to pray for Chloe.*

After class was over and people were breaking up, I went to Chloe, and I told her, "I feel like God is telling me I should pray with you. Do you need prayer?"

"In reference to what?" Chloe asked.

"I don't know," I said, because I truly didn't. God hadn't told me that part.

Chloe glanced around at the people still clearing out of the room. "Let's talk...after."

A few minutes later we were walking toward our cars, and we were trying to decide if we would pray right then, or if we should make an appointment for later, and Chloe just starting breaking down crying.

"...I do need prayer," she said. "I am in a horrible situation. Nobody knows about it...and I could really use your help."

I remember thinking, *Wow, God. You are so amazing...*

Chloe, now bawling, tried to gather herself together, but it was no use. "I so need help...I'm a closet drinker, and people don't know it...Oh, Misty I'm addicted to drugs. Addicted! My family has no idea...my husband...it would kill him...Misty... I've even thought about suicide...I just can't keep on doing this."

I didn't know all this at the time, but Chloe had gone through breast cancer, and through that experience had become dependent on pain pills, which in turn started her drinking. So here was a strong Christian woman, a wonderful wife and mother, an incredible person, that now found herself locked in a spiral she never saw coming. Her husband was a prominent man in the community, and the shame of thinking that this might be made public and reflect on him was too much for her to bear. So in her fear, she drank more. And in her shame of drinking, she took more drugs.

And this wonderful child of God was now locked in a very dark place, alone, with seemingly no way out.

But God had other plans for her, specifically...and I got to be a part of them. He was giving me a role. A responsibility in the battle of Light and darkness...Life and death. What an incredible honor. *Thank you, Father.*

We prayed right there on the spot, for strength and clarity and direction for the situation, and it became evident that this meeting wasn't the full extent of what God had in mind. "Okay," I told my friend, "We need to pray more. More than just here. Come to my house in three days and let's pray through this together." I asked for the three days because I wanted a chance to fast before she came.

I knew that God intended for me to pray with Chloe to get rid of demons. She needed to be delivered. He had so beautifully set me up for this moment that it was obvious. But it was still very scary. I had gone from not really knowing, or not really even considering, that demons could interfere with a Christian to having an undeniable experience of feeling one get up and leave right off of me. I mean, it was like…well, you get the picture.

Anyway, now here we were. This was all new and odd and a whole lot scary, but I knew what God was telling me to do.

And here's the only reason I was so certain: because I was hearing Him clear as a bell! I had a great confidence, because I was paying attention to the little things, like the fact that God told me to pray for Chloe out of the blue, and at that moment she was really needing prayer. I didn't discern that when I saw her that day, she didn't walk into the room looking like she needed prayer. God revealed it, and I acted on it, and it reaffirmed the fact that yes, indeed, I was hearing God and He had plans of His own, which He could now include me in…because I was listening!

So even though I didn't know how to do it, or what to do, or what to expect, I knew I had to invite her to come to my house and pray. I was excited that God was going to use me and she was going to get help. But at the same time I was thinking, *Holy moly God, I would never have chosen this! Deliverance? Really?*

Nevertheless, I was excited. I knew she was going to be free, because I was beginning to have a whole new understanding of God's desires, and our capabilities when we partner with Him. I knew that an ugly spirit had left me, which reassured me that the same thing could happen for her. I don't think God wants this stuff to be difficult…he truly does want us to discover these free gifts, and walk in freedom.

"I feel like you need deliverance," I told her. "I just learned about it and just went through it, so I'm still new at this, but I'm willing if you are. Let's pray and get you free from this."

Now don't get me wrong: even with the confidence that the

Creator of the Universe was walking me through this, I was still scared stiff. I got straight in the car and immediately called Dee. "Oh, my gosh, Dee, I need your help!" I told her about what had just happened with Chloe and the meeting we had set up. "I've never done this before!"

"Don't worry," Dee said. "I'll come be with you. We'll figure it out together."

The day Chloe was coming over to pray, I was a wreck.

I was scared, I was shaking. I had read the book Dee gave me and it had given me a foundation of what to expect. I don't want to freak you out, but this book talked about demons slamming people against the wall and things like that. This "spiritual struggle with the forces of evil in heavenly realms" stuff didn't seem like it was for lightweights.

But I was okay. I had heard God, so I knew He was with me in this. And I had Dee coming over, so I wouldn't be going it alone. As long as I had someone to go through this with me...

Well, a half hour before our meeting time, Dee called and said she had an emergency in her family, and she needed to get to the hospital. There was no way she could make it. I immediately thought about calling Chloe and rescheduling, but realized she was already on the way. Now my nerves went into overdrive. I was pacing the living room, praying.

Father...Father...Father...

But there was no turning back, and I knew it. Looking at it today I can plainly see that this was exactly how God wanted it, but at the time...I was a nervous stinkin' wreck!

Chloe showed up and she was even more of a mess than I was. She had alcohol on her breath from a heavy night of drinking. Knowing that she was coming, she had put herself through a really rough night. I realize now that demons know when they are headed for a fight, and they do anything they can to get a person to back out. They will try to cause headaches, sickness, embarrassment, or even convince the person that what they were going to pray about is really not that big of a deal, that they can deal with it on their own.

"It's been a horrible last couple of days..." Chloe mumbled. She let me know that she had been having dreams of ugly green slimy stuff overtaking her, trying to pull her down into somewhere dark. All she had been able to do was keep singing "Jesus loves me, this I know." Through the midst of it she saw what looked like Michelangelo's hand reaching down and gripping her, and she had spent the entire night feeling like she was being torn apart, caught right in the middle of this all-consuming battle.

"Okay," I said, trying to appear way more confident than I was. "Let's get started."

Please understand this: I had absolutely no clue what to do, other than pray. So that's what I did. We sat down on the couch and I started praying for the spirits to leave her. I would sometimes pray in tongues and sometimes pray in English. As I prayed, the knowledge would come to me where to put my hands. I would know when to lean in and whisper, when to stand up and be forceful and take authority. I just kept praying, laying my hands wherever the Holy Spirit told me to put them, and speaking whatever He told me to speak, and the next thing I know she started being delivered, in a massive way.

Hold on, let me correct that: IN A MASSIVE WAY.

Please don't let this freak you out...don't read this far and bail on me. If you have made it with me this far, God has you here for a reason. Trust Him.

Anyway, Chloe was arching her back, and sounds were coming out of her that...let's just say we were way past chit-chat. She was making the most horrible faces and noises, and during this time God just took over. It was unbelievable. Now that we were into it, I had absolutely no fear, because I realized that this was not my show. I wasn't responsible to get this done. It was God's show, and all He had needed me to do was just show up. As long as I kept allowing Him to do whatever He needed to do, through me, I didn't have to worry about whether or not I was doing what I should be doing. That's so very important: this wasn't about Misty doing the right thing, or even having any clue what to do next...because I surely didn't.

So this went on, and on, (at this point I was really glad we didn't try this in the parking lot) until one point where Chloe was pulling at her throat, saying she couldn't breathe. Finally, after what seemed like way too long, the highest, loudest, scream I have ever heard in my life began to come out of her. From way down inside, like an animal scream...

This book is not the place to go too deep into this. Just let me say that at the time I didn't understand the true authority I carried, and didn't understand that demons are basically just big bullies. They, too, are under the authority of Jesus Christ, as ALL authority in heaven and on earth has been given to Him. In deliverance sessions since then I have learned I can put limits on their acting out. But at this time, I had no idea I could do that.

When the first round of crazy stuff was over, Chloe sat there almost in shock. For quite a while she didn't say anything. Finally, gradually, she began to focus in on me. "Oh my gosh, that was real! Misty, something just left my body...I can't explain it, I feel lighter right now...you just don't understand...that was real!"

But I did understand. *Oh, thank you, Father. You are so amazing.* I did understand…perfectly, in fact…what it felt like for something to get up and leave my body.

God began giving me words to speak to her. They just started coming and I would speak them. In the midst of all this, He wanted to tell her (through me) that she was beautiful, and that He loved her, and that her husband loved her, and that the reason her husband wasn't touching her was not because he thought she was ugly, but because he was afraid he would hurt her. (As a result of breast cancer she had undergone a painful double mastectomy.)

Amazingly, God was revealing things to me, to speak to her, that I had no way of knowing on my own. Things she and I had never discussed. But as long as I kept speaking, God kept giving me the words. And no matter whether they made sense to me or not, I didn't question and I didn't hesitate…I just spoke whatever I heard Him say. This was the first time I actually prophesied. It was amazing some of the beautiful things God wanted to tell her.

It was obvious that the largest part of my role here was to just stay out of the way. To keep Misty out of it as much as possible. I mean, think about it: can you imagine how quickly the old Misty could have shut this down, through doubt, unbelief, or even fright? Or worse yet, a perfect plan? What a precious thing God would have been prevented from doing, if I had jumped in with some carefully-planned agenda.

In all, this was about a three hour session. We would talk, and pray, and go through some battles, and then talk, and then pray some more. God began to give me knowledge of which demon we were going after, and I would call it by name and command it to leave by the authority of Jesus. We went through discouragement, deceitfulness, depression…and no, not all demon's names start with "d," those are just the ones I remember right now.

Somewhere along the way, God gave me knowledge that what we were ultimately after, way down at the root, was the spirit of abandonment. Again, things I couldn't possibly know: Chloe's father had abandoned her when she was little, and God had me reveal to her that this was the root of many of the issues. As He worked through this, God assured Chloe that He was with her and He would never leave her.

While the first meeting was huge and dramatic, it didn't stop there. Over the next few weeks and months Chloe and I continued to have regular ongoing sessions, and she would go deeper and deeper and realize more and more healing. We'll talk more about that later.

So, all of a sudden, I have a deliverance ministry. I didn't see that one coming. I mean, I still didn't have a clue what I was doing. And while this was all new and exciting, (just trying to be real here) when God promised I would have a new ministry, this wasn't what I had pictured.

But I knew God...and I trusted Him. He wouldn't have chosen me if I couldn't handle it. So together, we went forward.

CHAPTER 8

GO TO UTAH

Shortly after this I went back to Tennessee to visit my sister. I had to share with her all that was going on and it definitely had to be done in person. While she and I were praying together, I began speaking in tongues and the Holy Spirit came down heavy. Thick...like love soup being dumped on us from one of those huge restaurant soup pots.

I just kept praying, and all of a sudden God started moving my hands! I remember I had no clue what was going on, just that my hands were moving, and He was the one moving them. Of course, I could have stopped them, just like I could stop speaking in tongues or laying on hands or any of the other things the Holy Spirit prompts me to do. But just because I had the power to make it stop doesn't mean I was making it happen. I was surrendered, giving Him free rein.

One thing I have learned is that as soon as something

becomes a battle in your mind between yourself and God, He will generally let you have your way. If God prompts you to deliver a word to someone, He won't make you do it. If He tells you to lay hands on someone, it's still your choice. He will never take away your free will; but He will ask and wait for you to yield your will to His.

So, anyway...he was moving my hands, and I didn't stop them. I just let them do whatever it seemed like they wanted to do. Sometimes, it seemed so funny! He would place them on my cheek as if I were precious. My fingers would make circles in the air, and then swing from horizon to horizon, like the sun coming up and going down. He would put my hands on my hips and have me make a pouty face...I'm telling you, sometimes I would just stop and crack up. But overall, somehow, the entire thing felt...holy. There was no doubt whatever my hands were doing, He was in it.

God is a lot of things, but He's not boring!

After I came back from Tennessee, one of my friends from church, Traci, came over and we were praying about a business situation she was trying to resolve. I really didn't know Traci at this point, other than from our (very traditional) Sunday school class, so she had not yet been introduced to the more... unusual...side of my praying. What I'm saying is I was keeping it pretty low-key, mindful of the knowledge that this was not the kind of thing we discussed in our church. I was keeping it to myself until I knew how to present it to people.

Anyway, there happened to be a man putting on a convention the weekend after next in Utah and the Lord said we needed to go see him, and it had something to do with the business dilemma she was trying to resolve. Traci and I both received that message very clearly. The Lord said, *Go to Utah*.

Mind you, we were in Sarasota, Florida. And we weren't rich. We weren't normal world travelers. But the Lord said *Go to Utah*, so she and I got on a plane and went to Utah. We took our airline miles and our hotel points (my husband had traveled for work in the past, so we had points saved up) and scraped together a little money and we were gone.

As a side note here, let me say: nothing feels better than to do something crazy for God! When you know you've heard Him, and it makes no sense, but you trust Him, and just as important, trust yourself that you're hearing Him…there's no greater feeling in the world. I stood in that airport waiting to board that plane with my Holy Spirit singing inside of me. I wasn't worried about where the money was coming from, or what my husband and the kids would do while I was gone, or any of the thousand things the world would try to convince me to worry about.

I was going to Utah. I had heard my God.

In the hotel room the next morning, I wanted to pray. Ever since this experience had started, the urge to pray had consumed me. It was my food, my water, my fuel, my sunshine. My strength and my rest. It was the place I wanted to be more than any other place in the physical world. Traci was still sleeping, and I went out on the eighth-floor balcony and just absolutely got lost in the wonder of the Holy Spirit. My hands were dancing, my tongues were flowing, my Spirit was singing, and suddenly the Lord stopped me right in my tracks.

Go show Traci, He said.

Oh, no, I thought. *Please, Lord…*

You can do it.

Ohhhh, crud…

So I went inside, and slid the door closed behind me. I eased over and rocked Traci real gently, thinking maybe she wouldn't wake up. But of course she did.

"God wants me to show you this," I mumbled, and then I went right back to where I was outside, tongues flowing, hands moving.

Traci sat straight up in bed. "Oh my God!"

"Yeah…I know." I thought she was going to tell me it was the most ridiculous thing she'd ever seen.

"I understand what you're saying!"

This caught me by surprise. "You do?"

"Yes!" Traci's hands moved to her face, which still had a look of shock. "Oh my God…I can't believe this stuff is real…I mean, I completely understand…that's so weird…you're praising God, and the Holy Spirit is saying He is so pleased with you, and…"

She went on to tell me all kinds of precious things I don't specifically recall anymore. After a short while she asked, "Do you know why your hands are moving?"

I just stared at her. "No, not really."

"It's like…a sign language from the Lord," she said. "You should start paying attention to what they do."

This was a huge revelation for me, and helped to clarify even more the things the Holy Spirit was telling me. Understand, my interactions with the Holy Spirit are not just hearing a voice within me. He pairs this voice with other things, such as hand movements and visions, and together they mean certain things. As an example, He frequently shows me people's feet, in the sense that they will be either straight, or pointing sideways, or turned completely around.

If I'm praying with someone He may show me (in a vision) their right foot is straight, but their left foot is turned around, and I will understand there is something about the situation that they are not seeing correctly, or thinking correctly about (turned around). As we pray and God reveals the truth He wants them to know, and they begin to understand the truth of the situation instead of the lie, He will then show me that their foot is turned back around the right direction.

An important point for me to relate is this: in all my years of meeting and talking with other people who are led by the Holy Spirit, none of them have ever told me that they see people's feet the way I do, or move their hands during prayer the way I do. God created each of as individuals, and we can fully expect that He will communicate to each of us in our own individual way. What He does with me makes perfect sense, to me. It's a closeness and a bond that He and I share. It's a language that He has taught me from His heart, not a language I learned by reading a book about how the Holy Spirit talks.

Anyway, Traci and I spent most of the next three days on the hotel floor, praying, learning, listening, and praying some more. Between what God was telling me and what God was giving her, there was so much to explore! We found that every layer we peeled back would reveal ten more.

We would pray for a while, then God would send us outside, and we would make our way down the street and pray for people we ran into. The Holy Spirit was giving us amazing insights and revelations into exactly who to pray with, and exactly what to pray about. People were amazed as we zoned in on the exact issue that they were facing, when sometimes they hadn't ever told anyone else about it! God gave us so many encouraging words for people that weekend.

But the whole time we had our minds on meeting this speaker. God had told us to see him and we didn't have a clue how. So we were asking everyone we ran into who was associated with the convention if there was any way we could speak to him. Finally, after at least a dozen people, we ran into a lady who was very closely associated with him, and she promised us she would relay the message, but she couldn't promise he would agree to see us.

Sometime later we were sitting in our hotel room and there was an urgent banging on the door. When we opened it, the lady was standing there, out of breath. "Okay! He's in between sets and he can see you, but it's gotta be right now!"

So the three of us took off running toward the convention center. She led us down this crazy route, through the kitchen, and finally told us to stand in a small area in the back hallway. After a few minutes he showed up, having stepped right off the stage. He was obviously exhausted, and the nurturing Mom in Traci took charge. "Misty, let's get this man some water and a sandwich!" she said, suggesting he sit down and relax.

Luckily we were already near the kitchen, and I was back in a flash with the water and sandwich. By this time he and Traci were sitting on the floor, praying. It turns out there were some areas of great stress in his life at the moment, and he had not been able to work through them up to that point. God told him he should meet with us when the opportunity was offered, and the three of us ended up having a wonderful sweet time with God. When we parted ways, this wonderful man was thoroughly refreshed, and it wasn't because of the sandwich!

This really taught me that when God tells me to go somewhere, it's not always the same reason everyone else is going. Others were going to Utah to attend the convention, to soak in what this man had to give. But it turned out God had us going there to pour into his life. We had never met this man, and it was a miracle how God brought it together. What started out as a brief encounter ended up in a few hours of beautiful prayer.

It turns out this man just needed someone to talk and pray with. A lot of leaders have nowhere to turn and they are thankful when God sends someone safe, someone they can be real, and genuine, and open with. I was honored that God trusted us to fly halfway across the country to minister to this lovely man.

We never even made it to the actual convention. We were only there for the prayer time in the hotel and to minister to the gentleman giving the conference. The old, practical Misty would have freaked out about not following the plan...*God said go to the convention, we need to go to the convention! We came all this way, blah-blah-blah.* (The old, practical Misty could be a real drag sometimes.) But the new Misty was really starting to enjoy this new freedom and following the Holy Spirit. It was quite an exciting adventure!

It became obvious to Traci and I that the real blessing God had in store for us was found in the very fact that the two of us were alone, away from the world, for a little while. This allowed us the freedom to pursue all the new things that God was showing us, and gave us the unique ability to test it out on a bunch of complete strangers, without any of the normal pressures of worrying what people might think! The fact that He sent us to Utah for a convention we didn't even make it to was irrelevant.

It reminds me of the story in the Bible where God told Abraham to take his son Isaac to the mountain, and offer him as a sacrifice...basically, kill him. That was a very definite command, with no wiggle room in it, and Abraham dutifully set out.

He had heard God.

Thankfully, though, Abraham knew to put more importance on the immediate command of God rather than yesterday's direction. He remained open to hearing God on a real-time basis. And while he did not discount what God told him yesterday, he knew that what he heard from God this very moment was the thing that he must do. The end result would have been disastrous if Abraham would have stubbornly followed yesterday's direction and not allowed room for God to speak into his life on a minute-by-minute basis.

So it wasn't that important to the new Misty if we didn't make the convention. It was beautifully obvious we had come and discovered everything God had for us in that weekend. In fact, remember that business question that Traci and I were praying about when God told us to go to Utah? Well, we did ask the speaker, and it turned out he didn't know an answer. But flying back home, Traci sat next to another man on the plane...you can probably see this coming, right? This man had certain very specific business skills which allowed him to perfectly answer every question Traci had. He even had a business meeting with her later on that week.

As for me, the plane ride home gave me time to reflect on what an incredible trip it had been. By simply listening to God and being available to follow His lead, I had seen more and learned more than I would have ever thought possible. Some of it was uncomfortable, like sharing my prayers with Traci, but it taught me a great lesson about not hiding this new thing the Holy Spirit was doing from others.

I thought again of the new believers in Ephesus, who had not even heard there was a Holy Spirit. I wondered if I had been in the same boat, because while I had heard about the Trinity (no one ever referred to the Father and the Son without mentioning the Holy Spirit) I never really "heard" about the love, the power, the depth, the beauty, the freedom, the desperation, the fulfillment...the "more."

At this point I decided to never hold anything back from anyone who asked. I would never present a partial gospel, but would always talk about the FULL relationship when I talked to anybody about God. I would fully embrace the complete gospel. Even though I knew it might sometimes bring division, I would never again shy away from it.

The blessings that came from the baptism of the Holy Spirit and fire were just too great.

CHAPTER 9

UNSPEAKABLE JOY

When I returned from Utah, I finally had a chance to get together with my friend Laurie, who had been in Wisconsin for the summer. I am going let you hear this next section exactly as she tells it:

I remember Misty had read this book, and she kept telling me about it when we would talk on the phone. Well one day she calls me and she's talking like ba-ba-ba-ba-ba-ba! super-fast, super-excited, and she says, "OH MY GOSH, I just had the WOW most INCREDIBLE experience! It was OH MY GOSH amazing! Just asked to be FILLED! Laurie! FILLED! Oh my gosh, Laurie! Just ASKED and speak in tongues and Holy Spirit and BAM! and Laurie you wouldn't BELIEVE and prayer language came through and most uplifting and can't even put words to it and oh my gosh, oh my gosh, OH MY GOSH!"

And I truly didn't understand a single word, but all I

could think was...*Oh wow...I want some of that...*

So as soon as I got back in town Misty came over and I could see, yes, indeed, she was filled. Filled with something. Filled to overflowing with a kind of joy that was just...not normal. And I started smiling, because I was thinking, *Yes, Lord, oh, yes, Lord, that's what I want, right there! Give me some of that! I so need that!*

So we went into the living room and got right to it. We prayed for me to receive the baptism of the Holy Spirit and the gift of speaking in tongues. Misty prayed, and then I prayed, and then we would pray together, and then Misty would pray again.

And nothing happened.

There was no feeling, no special language, nothing. And I remember we were really praying hard. I was praying hard. I said, "God, I want this. I really want this. Please give me this joy, this gift. I believe, God, I believe!"

At one point I remember Misty telling me, "Just start talking, and it will come."

So, okay, I started talking.

And I'm talking.

And here I am Lord, I'm talking, and yep, I'm still talking...and it didn't come. Eventually I started to get frustrated. (Misty had forgotten to mention that she had prayed for it for days and nothing had happened...)

I began to think, *Why in the world would God not let me have this, if I'm sitting here fully believing, fully wanting, and fully asking for it? If my faith is not big enough, does that mean there's something wrong with me? How is it I*

can hear so strongly and so clearly from God for so long,
but on this one thing right here it doesn't happen?

The whole thing was becoming very upsetting, and I knew enough to know that frustration wasn't going to get us anywhere. But at the same time...I couldn't help it. Yes, I was praying for something I wanted, but my motives were not self-centered. At the very heart of it I knew this was something that the Father desired me to have; this was a gift from Him to me, and He doesn't play games with His gifts. I knew that He didn't withhold any good thing; that He gives freely and in abundance...so why was this being withheld?

And right about that time Misty spoke up: "God is saying that you need to go to the Jewish pastor, and ask for healing."

"Rabbi," I said.

"Do what?"

"He's a Rabbi, not a pastor. Jewish people don't have pastors."

"Well, whatever...but you need to go see him and ask for healing, and God says then you will speak in tongues."

Now, one part of this was actually not all that strange. My family had been attending a Messianic Jewish Temple lately. God had led my husband there, and we had grown to cherish the idea that as Christians we had been grafted into the Jewish family. It was a new experience for us that had really opened our eyes to the richness of the culture.

But, then, the other part of this was a little strange. You see, we had only been attending the Synagogue a short time, and I had yet to actually speak to the Rabbi beyond "Hello." I hadn't imagined that our first real conversation would be about this. Nevertheless, next Friday after service, there I was, standing in front of Rabbi Ron.

And he looked at me with the most sincere love in his eyes. "Yes?"

"Well," I started, "I don't know if this is gonna make sense, but..."

I could see my husband and family sitting off to the side, waiting for me. I started again. "Well..."

I noticed he had the most patient expression. *Oh, heck with it,* I thought, *he's probably heard it all before.* So I jumped in..."My friend came over because I wanted to speak in tongues and we were praying and she could speak in tongues and I couldn't speak in tongues and I wanted to speak in tongues and God told her to tell me to come to you and get prayer for healing so here I am..."

And of course by now I was bawling, and the tears were gushing as fast as the words. I don't remember specifically what I was crying about, other than I just cry all the time anyway, and during that season I was going through a massive amount of personal hurt in my life, and my wound factor was off the chart. On a scale of 1-10, it was a 50. I was so, so, unhappy. I had been carrying a lot of junk I had not resolved, and my life had truly gotten to the point where I couldn't see myself ever being genuinely happy again.

So I stood there. And I blubbered.

And God bless Rabbi Ron. He said, "Well...Okay..." And he started praying. Praying God's love, praying

God's peace.

"I see you in a field," he eventually said, placing his hand on my shoulder. "And it's beautiful. There are flowers, all kind of flowers, incredible colors, and they're blooming all over."

In my mind I could see the field. I was right there, I was right with him.

"This field is huge, and wide," he continued.

Yes, I thought. I could see it, right there.

"And I see you. You're standing in this field...and your hands are raised up over your head..."

I could see my hands raised over my head...standing in the field...

"And you're on your tippy-toes, and you're filled... with an unspeakable joy."

Bam.

My heart sank. Because I knew...*That can't happen.*

I didn't say it, I didn't tell him that...I didn't ever tell anybody that... but I just didn't see myself experiencing that kind of happiness again. Ever!

"Thank you for saying those words," I said, stepping back. As we walked out, all I could think was, *It's a nice thought, but it would take a God-sized miracle. It's just too big. It's just too far.*

The next week I was at Misty's house and we prayed again for me to receive the baptism of the Holy Spirit. I had been asking for it pretty much constantly since the first time Misty came over. And when it hadn't happened then, and it hadn't happened since praying with Rabbi Ron, I went into a really bad place. It seemed like the only thing this whole episode had done was stir up all the junk in me I had been trying to just keep down.

But evidently God had declared this day to be different.

While we were praying, I was overtaken by an incredible rush of emotion. The best I can put it is there seemed to be a dam that burst inside of me, and it came. It came so hard that there was no question whether or not I could stop it or control it or contain it, even if I wanted to.

And, strangely enough...I started forgiving.

Speaking it, out loud, forgiving different people for whatever thought was there. Whatever came up, I immediately covered it with forgiveness and released it. There were some things I expected and some things that surprised me, but either way it didn't matter. I didn't let myself weigh every thought to see whether forgiveness was warranted. I just kept speaking forgiveness out loud, and the dam kept breaking, and this incredible rush kept coming.

And of course I was doing the ugly cry.

As I kept going, kept speaking it out loud, in English... all of a sudden...it wasn't. Somewhere along the way it changed, and the prayer language happened. It wasn't something I was trying for or looking for or even expecting, but there it was, and it was so incredibly beautiful.

I remember Misty telling me her experience was really fun, and joyous. But for me, it was a boatload of hurt and anger and betrayal and bitterness and confusion that all came up in a rush. Things down inside that were buried so deep I'd forgotten they were there…it all got covered with a forgiveness that only God could manage, and it all got released. It came up, and went out, and was gone.

My experience might not have been fun, like hers… but it sure was powerful. And it was very cleansing. And exactly what I needed.

Many times since that day I have thought back to Rabbi Ron's prayer. And every time I go and pray with someone, and see the Holy Spirit move in a powerful way on their situation, I think: *Here I am…standing in a field… on my tippy-toes…hands up…*

Filled with an unspeakable joy.

Laurie's experience wonderfully highlights the importance of forgiving. In my ministry, I have found this to be one of the main areas that Satan uses to keep us in bondage, and not allow us to find freedom or move forward. By continually reminding us of what the other person has done, he can keep us locked in unforgiveness, making us captive to bitterness. We will be continually tormented, and end up with a broken and wounded heart.

But if we forgive, it immediately swings open the cage of bondage that we are in. I think of forgiveness as literally being the key to our freedom. The book of Isaiah tells us that the Lord wishes to "bind up the broken hearted, to proclaim freedom for the captives, and release from darkness for the prisoners."

In releasing the person who hurt us, we find release for ourselves. This is so important because it allows us to no longer be affected by what they have done. Being bitter toward someone gives them a form of power over us, and by forgiving we finally get to take our power back. We can then hand the whole thing over to God, and once we turn it over we can rest, knowing that He will handle it in the perfect way. All pressure and responsibility is off of us, and we can focus on our own healing.

What confuses many people is the belief that if they forgive, they are letting the other person off the hook. Or even worse, they are saying that what the other person did was okay. But that's not what forgiveness is about, at all. It's not about the other person...it's really about the person who is doing the forgiving. When I forgive someone, I am giving myself permission to no longer be controlled by whatever they did. It allows me to be in control, and from that point I can begin the healing process.

It is my free choice to forgive. It is my choice to no longer be a captive to whatever happened. When I make that choice, it is important that I speak the words out loud, because my words...and your words...are living, and have power in the supernatural realm. Life and death is in the power of the tongue. So for example, I say, "I choose to forgive Mr. Smith for stealing from me. I choose to forgive him for taking away my family's retirement," or whatever the situation may be.

In the beginning our spoken words might not even feel like we're speaking truth. Say them anyway. Trust God that victory will come. I have had times when the first round of forgiveness was spoken through gritted teeth, and that's okay. Even if I don't feel like forgiving yet, it's important that I speak those words into being. It's important that the devil knows that I'm not playing around; I'm taking my power back.

Sometimes we have spoken the words of forgiveness, and know there should be freedom, but there's not. It may take days, weeks, and in some cases longer before the peace comes, but don't give up. It will come. We can develop triggers from past hurts which cause automatic responses within us, and we have to bring truth into those hurts in order to see complete freedom. Each time we feel the trigger, which may be once a day, or once a week at first, it's important to immediately speak out loud the words of forgiveness. As we do this, the Lord will bring truth into our hearts and reveal deeper levels of understanding of the true nature of our hurt. More and more truth will be continually introduced into the situation until one day there will be a release. The root will be cut off and the trigger will be gone. In other words, we will be free!

Forgiveness can be a process, but it is so worth it. Nothing can compare to walking in freedom, and it is what God desires for us. Our ability to forgive others truly is a gift from God, and it carries with it a beautiful promise: we will be set free. We will be able to move on to a life with freedom and peace.

CHAPTER 10

THOSE CRAZY LADIES THAT PRAY

———— ❧ ————

Laurie had returned from Wisconsin and been baptized in the Holy Spirit right before school started. Our children were attending the same school, and she and I showed up near the end of summer at an orientation that they put on.

There was another lady there who I really didn't know, but she was a good friend of Laurie's. Unknown to me, they had spent some time talking about this crazy deliverance stuff that had been happening in my life. Anyway, I ended up next to this lady at the orientation, and was trying to make small talk, when I commented on the fact that one of her children was not going to be attending the school.

And out of nowhere she spun around and absolutely unloaded on me! She demanded to know exactly what I was implying, and told me I didn't know what I was talking about, and how dare I say…

I was absolutely horrified. She stomped off and I was sitting there in shock, racking my brain trying to remember what in the world I had done to make her so angry. I actually went out into the hallway with tears filling my eyes. I was thinking, I hardly even know this lady!

Well, don't you know, the next week it happened that we both volunteered to be helpers at the school. I was in the restroom, and…you guessed it. She walked in. I stood there washing my hands, being very careful not to make eye contact. She seemed to avoid me for few seconds, then stepped right in front of me as I went to walk out. I remember thinking, *Oh please God oh please God oh please please please God.*

She looked me directly in the eye, and said, "Last night the Lord told me you would heal me, and I promised Him I would talk to you today if you were here. I have a demon, and I need to know if you will pray with me."

I was beyond shocked. I think I said something like, "aa-rrr-uuh-buh-buh?"

Nevertheless, she went on to let me know that she knew when this demon had come in and how long she'd had it. When she saw me that day she knew she was supposed to ask me to pray with her, but she admitted she was agitated about the whole thing and didn't know why. But she had asked God to provide an opportunity to talk to me, and now here we were in the restroom. Alone. Together. So she was asking me.

I have since come to realize that the agitation, the nervousness, the frustration that doesn't seem to make sense, is something that often happens in a person when they are finally at the point where they're going to get help. It's like the demons know the end is coming for them, and they start putting up a fight. But at this time I was still very green in all this stuff, and I was still a little nervous thinking that she was going to unload on me again. So, brave soul that I am, I managed to say, "Okay. We'll do it at Laurie's house."

Now, the old Misty was Mrs. Organization. Mrs. Preparation. It had only been a month or so since I had met with Chloe, and remember, during that incident I just showed up. However, now, with this lady…I just kept thinking, *What if I don't do it right? What if I screw up?* My gosh, I didn't even want to think about it…

So I determined that this time I was going to be ready. I headed straight home, got out all my books and my Bible, and went to highlighting and making notes and big red stars in the margins like crazy. I assembled three pages of Scripture references, and I mean I was three-hole-punching and color-coordinating and notebook-stuffing like a woman with a mission. I was going to be on top of it this time. I was going in with a plan, and it was a good one.

The day came for the prayer session, and when I pulled up at Laurie's house I knew exactly what I had to do. I was going to start by praying over the house, and then move into anointing each person with oil, followed by specific scriptures of preparation I had highlighted in my notebook. Mrs. Organization was in the house! I was on top of this one!

When I first walked into Laurie's home, I felt God tell us to join hands and pray. As soon as our hands touched…BOOM!

The Holy Spirit came down in force, Laurie and I started speaking in tongues, and the next thing I knew this lady was just being massively delivered. This went on for hours, and it had nothing to do with my plan. All my books, my notes, and everything I had prepared never even made it off of the kitchen counter. All God needed me to do was show up, and He took it from there. This was His plan, not mine. This was His day, and His time, and His show. Things go so much better when we remember this.

Evidently when God had spoken to this lady about praying with me, He was done with the waiting. He wanted her free, and wanted to leave no doubt that it was His work, not mine. This was a great lesson, and reinforced in me that this was not supposed to be a formula. This was supposed to be me, showing up when and where He said, and serving as a vessel for Him to work through. And when God says it's time to get it done, I don't need to worry about the details. I just need to expect incredible things.

It was beautiful. There was so much freedom given to this precious lady and we became amazing friends after this. Again, you never know how a friendship is going to be found or going to be started, but when God is involved you know it's going to be good.

As a side note, five days later she started speaking in tongues.

This lesson served me well a week or so later. I'm still amazed at how wonderfully God sets us up, revealing some new thing right before He calls on us to put it into practice. He truly is for us, and not against us. He deeply desires for us to have radical success when it comes to the supernatural battle that is going on. Remember, even though we spend our days going places and doing things in the physical, the battle we are called to fight is not against flesh and blood; the real battle is against the principalities, against the powers, against the rulers of darkness of this world. Against spiritual wickedness in high places. God takes this stuff seriously, and He is looking for soldiers who will join Him.

Anyway, my kids and a group of their friends, including Traci's kids, had been praying for a boy named Daniel, who had leukemia. Our church had a special weekend event where they were all praying for him, as well as people all over the world. I got a call from Traci, and she told me we needed to go pray with Daniel. It turned out that they had been fasting for this young man for two days, and Traci shared with me a dream she had the night before:

> In the dream, someone that seemed like Daniel's mother showed up and said "Come with me or he will die." At the time I didn't understand how we were supposed to get there, only that we had to get there. She took me by the hand and the next thing I knew we were in Daniel's bedroom, at which point she disappeared.

> I kneeled to pray and immediately heard God say, "Get up. He's behind you."

> When I stood up and turned around, a spirit slammed me back against the wall and started to attack me. I cried out for Jesus, and commanded the spirit to be removed. Angels began to appear, and they were pulling this thing off of me. I saw his back split open, and thousands of spirits were popping out. Instantly more angels appeared on either side, and they were grabbing these spirits as soon as they came out and were throwing them into the corner of the room.

> I realized while all this was happening that spirits were grabbing Daniel, and had already pulled him off the bed and were dragging him into the corner. He was clutching his blanket, and I grabbed ahold of the blanket as it slid across the floor to try and stop them.

> Suddenly I jumped up and declared Daniel healed.

I knew he was healed. And the next thing I knew I was back in my bedroom.

The next day, Traci's legs and stomach had red marks on them. It looked like a cat had scratched her...and she doesn't have a cat. She told me that she knew she was supposed to talk to this boy's mother, and we needed to go see him and pray for healing.

The first problem: we didn't know the boy's mother. The second problem: this was really freaking both of us out. Neither one of us felt comfortable about what we knew we had to do. Other than talking to Chloe in the parking lot one time, all of this...stuff...had so far been kept out of the church. We were both clear on the fact that it was unmentionable.

"Just call the church and see if you can find out who his mother is," Traci said, "if you can get her number, I'll talk to her."

That seemed to give me the easy end of the deal, so I picked up the phone and called my friend Terri who worked in the church office.

"Hey Terri, this is Misty, and I was wondering if I could get the number of the mother of that boy with leukemia."

"Why?"

Well, shoot...I had really hoped to avoid details. "I just want to talk with her."

"Well...What would you say to her?"

Now this was really odd. I didn't know Terri very well but I still didn't expect this level of resistance. It didn't make sense. Part of me just felt like saying "never mind" and telling Traci we needed to find another route. But I already had Terri on the phone, so I pressed on. "Well...Traci had this dream, and in this dream there were words that she was supposed to give to this boy's mother."

Terri was silent for a moment. Finally she said, "Well, Misty, he's not staying with his mother. There's a long story there. He's actually been staying with me."

"Then you're the one we're supposed to talk to!" I said, making a mental note of how good God is at arranging "circumstances." I hung up and relayed this information to Traci, who immediately called and explained the dream in detail to Terri. Traci told her about the fight with the demons, and about Daniel being pulled into the corner, and how she eventually knew that he was healed.

Terri listened to the entire story, and then said, "He's still sleeping today. When he gets up I'll talk with him and see what he says, and then I'll call you back."

When she did call me back (which felt like forever), I merged Traci into the call. Terri sounded excited, and told us Daniel had agreed to see us. It turned out when he got up Terri casually asked how he had slept, and he had initially told her fine. Terri didn't say anything about Traci or the dream, and was a little disappointed that there was nothing to confirm the battle Traci had experienced. However, a little while later Daniel came back and said, "There was one weird thing about last night: when I woke up, all my covers were shoved into the corner of the room, and I have no idea how they got there."

At this point Terri felt more certain than ever it was spiritual warfare.

We hung up, so excited. And so scared. Excited because we knew God was doing something big, and we were right in the thick of it. He had wanted to relate something important, and we had caught it. And scared...because this was just scary stuff. Covered with scratches and blankets piled up in the corner? At what point was this dream more than just a dream?

We set up a time to see Daniel and prayed about who should go. It turned out to be myself, Traci, and Laurie. We felt led to fast a few days, and when the day came we were still all very nervous, but by now had adopted the philosophy of *God, we're just going to show up, and trust that you will do whatever you want to do.*

When we got to Terri's house, it was an agonizing site. Daniel's skin was gray. His eyes were yellow, and his body was nothing but bones. I felt led to just start speaking over him in tongues, so that's what I began to do. God told Traci to lay her hand on his lower back, at a spot where—in her words—a lady really wouldn't want to put her hand. She said later that when she did, it felt like her hand just stuck there.

The room was full of people...the three of us along with Terri, her husband, and her son who was Daniel's best friend. The Holy Spirit had Laurie ask Daniel to just start confessing, whatever came to mind. It began relatively peaceful, but it sure didn't take long for things to get heated up. All I can say is that the entire next several hours were filled with wild, wild, warfare. The three of us were battling, speaking God's Word, declaring, praying in tongues, doing whatever God told us to do in the moment. Other people in the room began manifesting, with spirits coming out of them, even though we tried to keep our focus on Daniel.

I guess God figured He was getting a package deal! We would be doing spiritual battle over Daniel, and turn around and there would be someone needing prayer in another corner, so one of us would go and pray over them. We learned that there are reasons not to do this in a full room when you're not used to it... the whole scene was loosely-controlled chaos!

By this time we didn't know what to think. God would swing back and forth from periods of very loud, very strong battle, to periods of soft gentleness, where He would give Daniel words through us about his future and the plans He had for him. He would spend a while with Daniel, and then direct us over to one of the other people in the room, and spend some time prophesying about their future. And then we would head back into warfare...he would have us speak with authority, forceful words that only God could understand.

There was a point during this warfare, this casting out of demon after demon, spirit after spirit, calling forth whatever name God gave us, that Traci and I smelled an odd odor. We didn't dwell on it at the time but discussed it later. We both knew it was the spirit of death. It was definite and unmistakable. It had a stench that could not be anything but death.

When everything seemed to settle down for the final time, Traci's hand was still stuck to Daniel's lower back. It had been there this whole time. "I'm so sorry," she said. "I just can't move it."

"Do you know where your hand is at?" Daniel asked.

Traci shook her head no.

"That's where they gave me the bone marrow treatment."

And then, at some point...we knew we were done. We all kind of looked at each other and said, "Well, let's wait and see."

Daniel had already had a bone marrow transplant from his sister which hadn't worked, and the doctors had said the only thing left was just to make him comfortable. They gave him some minor chemo just to extend his life so he could go the following week on his Make-A-Wish trip to NYC. I found out later they only schedule this trip when they know it's over and there's nothing else they can do. Their plan was to try and keep the pain manageable long enough to give his family a sweet, memorable trip.

When we had shown up that day Daniel was dull, and gray, and everyone seemed to be just waiting for the end. When we left, his eyes were clear and white and his cheeks were pink in color. We had no doubt that he was healed, and we were looking forward to seeing a report from the doctor.

As we were driving home, Traci was very shaken up. "I do not ever want to do that again!"

All I could think was *Oh, God, that was so awesome!*

Laurie just sat in the backseat, thanking God. Praising Him for the opportunity. Praising Him for His greatness. Praising Him for allowing her to be a part of this experience.

When Daniel went on his trip, he actually called Terri and told her he felt really good, better than he had in a long time. He was still weeks away from his next blood test because of his insurance. When it finally rolled around, I can remember getting the phone call from Terri like it was yesterday.

She told me that the test came back and he was 100% leukemia-free! I remember screaming "Hallelujah" over and over on the phone, then hanging up and dancing like I've never danced before.

This was huge. I mean HUGE! It was the first time God had sent us somewhere to pray for healing, and we had witnessed a man completely healed of leukemia. This was a big deal! The confidence I received from this experience increased my faith ten-fold.

There was much celebration that day in Florida!

This next section is very difficult.

We kept in close touch with Daniel over the next few months, going back numerous times to pray with him. Terri informed us that the doctors believed Daniel was simply in remission, and that he should now move forward with a stem cell transplant with cells from his brother. They felt that this was their opportunity to do this additional procedure now that he was strong enough.

Of course, we knew no further procedures were necessary. God had declared it done. Even so, we were hesitant to tell Daniel not to do something that the doctors were urging him to do. We wanted Daniel to pray and hear God for himself. Even after the test results, it was hard for him to believe that a miracle had taken place. He was eighteen, and it's a lot for a young person to handle. Shoot, it's a lot for anyone to handle.

On one hand, we were certain he was healed. On the other, the doctors were certain he was in remission and required further treatment. And in the middle, Daniel was just very confused. Over there he had years of professional experience, and over here he had "those crazy ladies that pray." That's what his friends and many others in the church had begun to call us, now that word was getting around about our prayer ministry.

"Those crazy ladies that pray"…isn't that awesome? I love it. I'll bet it makes God smile, big.

As confusing as this had to have been for Daniel, it caught us off guard, too. This was all new for us, and it's scary to tell someone not to have a treatment that medical professionals are saying will save their life. But I can also imagine how difficult it would be for someone in the medical profession, with all of their schooling and all of their experience and all of their genuine desire to help the patient, to suddenly halt all treatment in the belief that there had been a miraculous healing. It would seem to them like they were giving up, going against their calling to do everything they could do to help, and just saying, "Well, we'll hope for the best..."

But we knew. He was healed. And the test results proved it.

At this point we just felt it was critical for Daniel to hear God himself. For him to experience the unmistakable voice of the Master Physician so he would find the confidence to stand on the seemingly impossible. We would pray that he would hear God say not to go forward with the surgery, that the healing was complete. When we prayed for him during that time our prayers were focused on the importance of him hearing God's voice and direction. We knew there would be more power in him hearing it directly from God rather than through us.

I never could find the boldness to go to Daniel and tell him exactly how I felt. Laurie did write a letter, and Traci and I took it to him and read it. The letter very plainly said that God was saying, *Don't do it. I healed you, and it's done. 100%.*

In the end, Daniel said that he felt like he needed to go forward with the procedure. He felt that if God opened a door, he needed to go through it. The operation took place, and unfortunately his body did not react well to it.

He died shortly after.

Daniel's funeral was beautiful. So many kids gave their life to Christ, and celebrated Daniel's life in such a sweet way. As we sat in the back and experienced it all there was such mixed emotions. We celebrated Daniel's memory, but we were also devastated, because we knew what God had planned for Daniel, and he didn't get to experience it. During our prayer session with him, we had been shown clear visions of him talking in front of thousands of people, in what seemed like Africa. At that meeting we had also prophesied over Daniel's friend that his music would be played on the radio, and today it is.

Many weeks after the funeral, my daughter told me Daniel came to her in a dream and told her he was so happy, because his job in heaven was making the swords that were used for spiritual warfare. In the dream, he actually gave her one. I was talking with Terri many years later and shared this with her. She was amazed, because her son had the exact dream around the same time my daughter did. It helped my heart to know Daniel was happy.

But I remember just sitting there at the funeral, thinking… *he's not supposed to be dead.*

And being honest here, I felt responsible for his death. As I sat there, I was sad. I was angry. I was disappointed in myself. This wasn't supposed to end this way. Had I let Daniel down? Should I have been bolder? Was he dead because I didn't have enough faith or courage to say, "Don't get the procedure! Do not do it!"

Or had the modern church let him down, by not talking enough about these topics in their services? If the subjects of healing and deliverance were more familiar, more commonplace among Christianity, would it have helped Daniel to more readily accept and embrace his own healing?

Please don't get me wrong, our church was rallying around him every day, in every possible way they knew. They were fasting, they were having fund raisers, they were making t-shirts...this church stepped up in a huge way, and I'm certain everyone involved was praying the same thing: be healed, in the name of Jesus.

But why was it so hard to accept when it happened?

When Daniel was healed, I think he knew down deep in his heart it was from God. But because a lot of the world around him didn't believe, it didn't give him a firm foundation on which to step, and take a stand. After all, it was a tall order to believe that God would use a group of crazy praying women to deliver a healing of such magnitude...or was it? Thinking about it, who else should He have used?

Would it have made a difference if the church had rallied behind the healing and supported it? I firmly believe that if the church as a whole were more open and educated, and the subjects of healing and deliverance were talked about as normal occurrences in the spiritual battle, then the subject of healing would not be so taboo.

This would allow everyday Christians the freedom to have the faith to accept this "craziness" as part of God's normal plan, and make them more ready to turn toward a supernatural solution with at least the same expectations as the next experimental medical treatment. I believe some pastors avoid these discussions because the topics can start arguments...but the focus on salvation alone comes at a great cost to their congregation.

After the test results came back, but before Daniel's death, God told me to go to our pastor and speak with him, and while there we discussed Daniel's situation. Among other things, I asked him why he did not preach about healing, casting out demons, and speaking in tongues from the pulpit.

His response was that he knew Daniel was healed. He

believed fully in healing, had seen people healed, and even had a friend who had seen someone raised from the dead. The pastor knew that speaking in tongues was of God, but his mission was to bring salvation to the lost, and that's what he concentrated on. I told him I thought it was unfair we didn't let people know that there was more, and began to relate to him the things that happened when I became Spirit-filled.

"Right there," he said. "That's it. You're saying you're Spirit-filled, so what you're saying is that you weren't filled with the Spirit beforehand. That terminology starts arguments in the church, and that's what I don't want to be a part of. My mission is salvation. You can do your ministry, in fact I fully support your ministry…I just don't want it during our services. You can go pray with anybody you want in the church, but it needs to stay outside of the pulpit."

When I took time to think it through, I sort of understood what he was saying. There was a time when if someone had told me I needed to be Spirit-filled, what I would have heard was that my relationship with God and Jesus wasn't good enough. Somehow it wasn't valid, or it wasn't real enough, when in fact even back then I knew it was 100% real.

So perhaps it would be more proper to say we had the relationship with the Holy Spirit but didn't understand the power, the fullness of what that entailed. Once we understand the authority God places within us, and the true power that Light has over darkness, it changes everything. Things are no longer like they were; they're not the same…regardless of how clumsily we try to describe it.

I'm not in agreement that a church should avoid teaching this solid Biblical truth just because they can't get the words right. In an attempt to avoid the terminology argument, I think I like to say that I'm Spirit-Activated. That's what the baptism of the Holy

Spirit with fire feels like for me. I feel like all of the gifts, all of the authority, all of the purpose that God created me to have in the spiritual realm have now been revealed and activated.

Looking back, the truth of the situation was that we had been obedient. There were so many things we learned. God had absolutely showed up that night...the power came, and a miracle took place. It's all very complicated and there's so much I don't know, but I do know this: Daniel was healed, and I would loved to have seen him in Africa, ministering to millions.

CHAPTER 11

REALLY, GOD?

By this time, largely because of what had happened with Daniel, my young ministry had reached an important point: I no longer freaked out, no matter what God hit me with.

I had come to realize that what God tells me would often feel awkward, at least in terms of logic, and common sense, and man's knowledge...in terms of the world. I was becoming more aware than ever that the world is not moving in God's direction; in fact, in most cases the world is moving in exactly the opposite direction. Unfortunately, too often the world does not listen for and discern God's direction, and follow Him. People follow instinct, feeling, habits, whatever.

But it makes perfect sense if you think about it, going back to everything we learned about God from our church and our Bibles. We're not supposed to be conformed to this world, but rather transformed by the renewing of our mind.

Since the baptism of the Holy Spirit, God was also revealing more and more spiritual gifts, in ever-increasing power. Over and over it seemed like He would set me up for the next big thing by introducing exactly what I was going to need to allow Him to deal with it when we got there...sometimes the week before, the day before, or even the hour before! In fact, as soon as I began to feel comfortable, He would bring something new— and it was so fun! This was such an exciting time in my life!

So I finally stopped being surprised and questioning when God told me something that made absolutely no sense. I might still laugh and ask, *Really, God?* But I would not hesitate. I would not fail to move forward on whatever direction He had given me, no matter how illogical it seemed. And I certainly would no longer run away. Because of this new boldness my ministry eyes were being opened to see more than ever, and my ministry muscles were being stretched to places I had never imagined they would go.

Life became a big Kingdom adventure. I would move through the day expecting constant interruptions from God, and He would never disappoint, telling me things like, *Go tell that person that their husband loves them,* or *Make a right turn at this next block,* or *Go pray with that person... I will give you the words when you get there.*

God was giving me dreams, and prophecy, and incredibly powerful and specific prayers. He was using spiritual warfare, and healing, and deliverance. While I began to be a little less surprised at some of the things He would tell me, it still amazed me that I was right in the middle of all the things I had run from just a short while ago. All of this wonderful ministry fruit, this yummy–yummy God relationship I had wanted so badly for so long, had been right on the other side of the legalistic, religious wall I had erected in my own mind.

The freedom I was now experiencing in simply walking and talking with God was taking me places I had never imagined. It was helping me to become a stronger, more fulfilled person. And for the first time, I finally felt like I was doing what I had been created to do.

One day I was in church and a group of us women were presenting our prayer requests to the class. There was one lady named Robin, who I really didn't know, who requested prayer for her daughter. It seems her daughter had been suffering from headaches for years, and they had become so bad that she was actually home from school, bedridden. Of course they had enlisted many different doctors to examine her, and there had been no progress whatsoever. The headaches continued to get worse, and were now truly disabling.

God told me to ask Robin if my friends and I could come to her house and pray over her daughter. I was excited, because by this time I knew when something like this was God's idea, He was ready to do something miraculous.

When I asked her she smiled, very genuinely, and said she would need to check with her husband to see if it was okay. Later that afternoon or the next day, she called me back and said, "Thank you, but my husband says no. I hope your feelings aren't hurt." I told her I understood, and my feelings weren't hurt. I just needed to be obedient and God had told me to ask.

Several months went by, and I would see her in passing, and I knew the word around church was that her daughter was getting worse. One day, she called me. I remember the exact conversation. She said, "Misty, we are desperate. I really need you to come and pray with my daughter."

Ohhhh, yeah...love that word. Desperate.

So like always, I prayed and asked God who should go with

me, and this time He said Traci. At this time God would usually send at least two of us. Traci got in the car that day, and I'll tell you what, she did not want to go. She jumped in the car already griping. She wasn't prayed up, she didn't feel worthy to go, she just all around didn't feel good about it. The only way I could get her to calm down a little was by telling her she only needed to go and sit there. Just intercede, and I would take care of all the rest.

It was becoming common that Satan would try anything to keep us from showing up at what was going to be a powerful session. Many times when we would schedule something, the day before we would feel like we were catching the flu, or some oddball thing that just had to be attended to would pop up, or any number of things that seemed so important at the time but looking back you realize…that was just the enemy. *Nice try, devil.*

Well, whatever it was that day, Traci was crawling with it. She was just fit to be tied. There was nothing in her that wanted to go. We pulled over in the parking lot of a grocery store on the way just to regroup, but she was still an absolute mess!

"I just don't know why God had me come!" she carried on. "I don't feel like I can do anything…I don't feel the Holy Spirit on me today…I'm not going to be effective at all!"

We eventually went on over to the house, and when Robin came to the door with a big smile on her face, she exclaimed, "I just know this is going to happen!"

Traci told me later all she could think was, *Oh this poor lady…she's going to be so disappointed.*

Nevertheless, we followed her inside and into the living room. By this time it had gotten to the point where the daughter had not been to school in four months. Her headaches had become so unbearable. The first round of doctors and the second round of doctors and the third round of doctors were at a loss.

The family was desperate. It was time for God to show up.

We joined hands in the living room and prayed with Robin, and after a few minutes Traci's demeanor suddenly changed. It was like flipping a light switch, it was that sudden. All of the negative whatever was gone, replaced by the presence of the Holy Spirit so thick you could feel it on your skin.

"Whew. He's here," Traci said. "Yep. He's here…okay, we can get started now."

God is so funny, He always has His own plan. He told me to take Robin into one room and for Traci to go into the daughter's bedroom. She told me the first thing God told her was to have the daughter start repenting, of anything and everything that came to mind. Repent, repent, repent. After that, Traci felt this incredible, almost electric, power in her hands and knew that she was supposed to lay them on the little girl's head. Needless to say, the change was immediate and dramatic.

Meanwhile, God had me praying with Robin. There were some wounds that she had from the past and God wanted to heal her of them. It was an incredible prayer session and she had a beautiful healing.

By the time we left that day, the daughter was up, and walking around, and smiling the biggest smile you've ever seen! Her mom's face was shining from the Glory of God and praising Jesus for her healing and her daughter's. We found out later that her daughter returned to school the following week, and soon after formed a Bible study for other students. Can I get an AMEN?

Another unique thing happened with this situation. We got a call from Robin a few days later, and she said that her daughter's headaches were 90% gone but there was about 10% still there. I got together with Traci and we prayed about this, and learned something very interesting: God said that He left the 10% so that the daughter would learn how to pray healing over herself, and if she would pray, the headaches would go away. This was necessary so that she could strengthen her own faith, and begin to know God better for herself. We called Robin and told her this and she relayed it to her daughter.

Sure enough, her daughter prayed and the headaches went completely away. A couple more times after that, it would seem like they would start to come on, but because she knew how to pray, she was able to quickly take care of it herself, and in a short time they were gone completely.

CHAPTER 12

BRING LIGHT INTO THE DARKNESS

So remember Chloe?

Throughout all this time she and I were still getting together, praying, talking, and spending time together. She had some incredible victories over her drinking and drug addiction, but there were still waves of depression at times. During one of these, she was at my house and we were praying. I began to cry out to God, and let Him know I was aching for His wisdom over this situation. I felt like I was in pain, like I could literally feel my heart breaking. (Sometimes God will allow me to experience what the other person is feeling.)

I was confused as to why complete victory was not there. Knowing His heart was for her to be free, and that He held all authority, why did her freedom seem so elusive? Why did it not last? Why did the depression keep coming back?

As I continued to cry out, I heard God say, very clearly... *There is a baby.*

It's silly, but as many times as I have heard God, now and then something about His voice will still surprise me. Maybe the directness, or the way it restructures everything in an instant. The shock of how quickly the darkness of a situation flees when light hits it. This was one of those times. Four simple words changed absolutely everything. I knew we had found our path, and I opened my eyes to ask Chloe if there was a baby, or something about a baby.

Without hesitation, she answered, "No."

"Well, God is definitely bringing up a baby. Do you know why?" I was becoming a little more bold these days.

"No. I don't know why."

"Did you have a baby die? Was there a miscarriage?"

"No."

I remember thinking...*There is a baby. God says there is. Father, what are you wanting to show us?*

"Have you had an abortion?"

"Misty, no...there's no baby."

""Okay," I said after a few moments, at a loss where to go from here. "Are you sure?"

"Yes."

I was certain God was saying something about a baby, and I even told Chloe I believed it was standing in her way of complete healing. I let her know I felt like we had hit a wall. She gathered her stuff and left the house, and for a couple days I didn't hear anything from her. But I thought about her, a lot. This time around I knew what I had heard, and I was so familiar with hearing God's voice I didn't doubt it was true. But that sure didn't make it any easier.

It was a long couple of days.

Eventually the phone rang. Chloe was crying, and very softly told me that yes, there had been a baby. There was an abortion. She whispered that nobody knew, not even her husband. She had experienced abuse and molestation at a very young age, and because of that she had become sexually active early, and had in fact gone through two abortions.

"That's okay," I told her, "Because God wants to heal and set you free from that."

And did He ever…it was so beautiful.

Chloe and I got together the next day and she was beautifully delivered from all of the lies surrounding the abortions. Not just the act of the abortion itself, but all the garbage that she was believing that went along with it. It was such a spider web, where it seemed like every false belief was connected to three others. She was holding on to these lies because she thought she had to in order to keep her family together, when in reality all they were doing was tearing her apart. When we were done, there was such great victory. There was perfect clarity in her mind and her heart, and a great hope for the future which had been missing for so very long.

Somewhere during the session God did the most amazing thing. And no, I'm not willing to argue theological details at this point, I'm simply going to tell you what happened. Over the course of about ten minutes, He took Chloe to heaven, and asked her if she wanted to see her babies. He told her that she could hold them, and allowed her to name them. He assured her that right now He was taking care of them, and that she would see them in heaven when the time was right.

At this point Chloe's eyes opened and her hands flew to her mouth, covering a gasp.

"What is it?" I asked.

It took her a little while to speak. When she did it was very soft…"What will they think of me?"

"Let's ask Father."

I had no idea what He would say, but I knew His heart, and I knew He would not be condemning. He would in no way hurt her. She had repented before the Lord, and He was ministering to her. We closed our eyes and she prayed to her father with this question. It was probably only fifteen seconds that passed, but it seemed much longer. Eventually a smile made its way through her tears.

"He says they will only know my love. They don't know what happened, and they don't hate me…they only know my love."

This released powerful healing for Chloe, and seemed to set a lot of things right in her mind. For the first time in a long time, Chloe believed she was deserving of God's love. We cried and hugged and laughed and cried some more. We praised God and gave Him the glory, and about this time He revealed one more thing: It was very important that Chloe tell her husband everything that had happened. She needed to bring it into the light.

"Oh, no!" Chloe said. "No…he'll think I'm dirty!"

And all of a sudden, after all of this wonderful progress, we again found ourselves at a standstill. I was certain that God was telling me Chloe must share this with her husband, and she was equally certain that it would ruin their marriage. Over the years, she had hid one thing after another until the pile of lies was so big she believed it couldn't be uncovered. It had grown unchecked for so long, that in her eyes it now held the power to destroy everything. She was absolutely, no question about it, not going to reveal any of this to her husband.

I was beginning to understand the importance of our words… the Bible says life and death are in the power of the tongue. Our words, spoken out loud, contain the very power of life and death, of freedom and bondage.

The abortions were the lie that was keeping her from complete freedom. I need to point out again that it was not just the fact that she had the abortions…that they had happened… too many issues stemmed from all of the garbage that she had piled up in her mind in order to "deal" with it. She had laid a firm foundation on a wrong belief, on a lie, and as a result Satan was able to start stacking the blocks higher and higher, lie on top of lie, until the whole thing became this strong, seemingly undefeatable tower.

Until that foundation was utterly and completely destroyed, Chloe didn't stand a chance of bringing that tower down. Of being cleansed and truly free.

This was a real eye-opener, because it gave me great insight into the deliverance ministry. Many times the things that are most obvious, right out in front of a person's troubles, are the things we attack and battle first. This reveals something else, and we go to battle with it next, and so on and so on. It can be very long and very exhausting. But these top-level things are often just symptoms of issues hidden deeper below, and if we ask God to uncover the foundation, the root, and take it out…the whole nasty lot usually falls away much easier. Deliverance for me became less exhausting the more I did it. I became more focused on finding the Big Lie rather than battling every individual little demon, and as a result the victories were quicker, deeper, and more complete.

With Chloe, we had prayed through a lot of junk, and experienced many victories, but she never found complete freedom until we dealt with the abortions. And to seal the victory, God had said she needed to reveal everything to her husband: the drinking, the drugs, and the abortions. She needed to bring the lies into the light. The fact that she was keeping them hidden allowed them to have power, and as long as they still held power, the easiest recourse for Chloe would be to try to numb herself with pills, with alcohol, with whatever.

Even after all of our sessions where she had been so powerfully delivered of so much, she was still struggling with staying free of pills and drinking. When she would share this with me, all I continued to say was for her to be truthful with her husband. Tell him everything, and only then could she go forward.

Now, God doesn't make us go back to every single person we ever lied to and come clean, but under this circumstance it was important for Chloe. Opening up to her husband and bringing the secrets into the light would give Chloe her power back, and allow him to offer his support and accountability. And eventually, she did tell him. One night I got a call and, crying, she said, "Misty, I don't know what I've done. He's going to leave me. Oh my God, I just know he's going to leave me."

And I will admit, it was tough.

It took her husband a few days to sort through it, to fill in the gaps and draw the connections. Remember, throughout all of this, the one thing she had done very well was hide it. Hide the abortions, the drinking, the drugs, the fear. Satan had her convinced that she had to carry this entire burden by herself, and for a while she had been pulling it off...but it was killing her. He had deceived her about the very thing God had provided to help her through the hard times, which was a strong godly man to walk beside her. Satan had convinced Chloe that in screwing up so bad she was now in this alone, and no longer entitled to that portion of God's blessing.

But it was not so. Yes, initially her husband had a very hard time with all of this news. But truth won out, and he eventually thanked her for telling him and their relationship grew stronger than ever. He was able to come along beside her and be her accountability partner, and she was able from that point on to be completely transparent.

And that transparency finally killed the power of the lies. Once the light had been shined on all the lies and secrets, the darkness had to flee. It lost its power. Chloe was healed and completely delivered. Her desire for drinking and pills was no more, because at that time there was nothing left to numb.

While victories like this are certainly incredible, they are rarely easy. This is difficult stuff. Satan doesn't just let go and give up. Truth and openness have a hard battle to fight in the middle of a fallen world with fallen people, full of so much fear and anger.

People will sometimes come out and respond with stuff that is so bad, so nasty, so mean, that all you can do is focus on God. But when we look at the big picture, at the battle that is going on in the supernatural realms, we begin to understand how much the devil has riding on his lies. It's truly the only thing he has. Once the lies are exposed and defeated, and God's people are able to walk in truth, God has the freedom to do incredible things.

Chloe went from hiding in darkness, terrified of being abandoned, terrified of being found out, to standing on stage boldly giving her testimony one year later. She spoke at a women's conference in front of two hundred ministry leaders, and gave her entire testimony, including the abortions. After she was done, many women, including pastor's wives, approached her and said, "Wow. I feel like now I can finally go home and tell my husband…"

Another fruit from Chloe's freedom is that she began volunteering at a pregnancy care center, which quickly became one of her new passions. Because of what she had been through, she was able to really connect with the women and keep many of them from having abortions. She knows that since she faced her past and was obedient to God, there are now beautiful children in the world that would not have been. She went from closet drinker and drug addict to the front lines of the battle, winning people to truth, and life.

When you bring the light into the darkness, Satan no longer has a hold. The darkness has to flee. When the darkness flees, the lies and the fear no longer have power and dominion over a person's life, and when people get their power back they come into their identity and begin to realize who they are in Christ. It's all about the power…God has it all, but we give it to the devil when we choose to believe his lies. Any dark secret we are holding gives the devil leverage which he can use against us. It gives him our power.

Abortion is a hard topic. Many girls are forced to go through it, or told it's no big deal, that it will make their life easier. But it is a big deal. And it needs to be dealt with, in the way only our loving Father can. Through repentance, forgiveness, and acceptance of God's loving mercy the devil can be denied a foothold. If it becomes a secret, wrapped in guilt and shame, and becomes something necessary to hide…something necessary to lie about…the devil has an opening, and he is never one to show mercy.

Supernatural powers are always present in every situation, and good is always battling evil. Choosing to believe the truth over a lie is one of the easiest ways to allow God control of a situation. Today, Chloe knows she will not be abandoned. Period. She has no more fear, because she is completely transparent. As long as she chooses to live in truth, the lies will have no power.

It's not always easy (although it becomes easier after you've had a few victories) but if you can just take that first small step you will be amazed what God can do with it. Chloe didn't want to do what she knew God was telling her to do. But once she did, it was amazing how quickly the whole mess was cleaned up. Not just removed, but replaced with something so much better.

But she had to stop hiding from it. She had to begin in faith, and the victories along the way gave her more confidence, more realization, that this was true. This was for real.

If we confess our sins, He is faithful and just and will forgive us our sins and purify us from all unrighteousness.

1 John 1:9 NIV

If you really want to experience the power of God in your life, you have to take that first step into the ugly stuff.

That's where the beauty is.

CHAPTER 13

DID THAT JUST HAPPEN?

I don't want to waste too much of this book talking about our enemy, but I do think it's important to recognize a few things. Satan does not want you to walk in your power. He will use fear and lies to keep you from knowing your identity and purpose. His goal is to stop you from living in your calling. If he can do that, he'll keep you from your destiny.

In my case, I have always had an unnatural fear of speaking in front of crowds. My neck would turn red, I would begin to shake, and get nervous to the point that nothing mattered but getting out of the spotlight. While this may be a completely natural anxiety I share with many people, in my case Satan has tried to take it to a level way beyond normal. Once I realized this, I stopped shying away from these opportunities to speak. My hands still shake and my neck still turns red, but I nevertheless go forward. I refuse to allow him the victory in this area, because I am convinced that this is his attempt to block a portion of my calling.

I am also naturally a very ordered and structured person. Looking back it is so obvious that the enemy made use of that for a long time, convincing me that anything that didn't make complete rational sense must not be of God. And just like the tower of lies that he built up in Chloe, he had built one in me against speaking in tongues. The only reason I eventually accepted it was because I began to hear God, and made the commitment to trust whatever He told me...even if it didn't make sense, even when it felt uncomfortable.

I think this is an important point to make: if you try to explain and make sense of all this within the confines of the natural realm, you'll get tripped up. You will restrict yourself from experiencing the fullness of what God has planned for you, because quite frankly what He has planned for you is going to happen mainly in the supernatural realm, even though it will have an effect in the natural. The splash happens in the supernatural, and we don't always see it with our physical eyes...with our natural eyes. In the natural realm we will only see the ripples that the splash creates.

This is one of the difficulties in writing a book like this. To go back and try to explain a lot of the things that happened, I can easily tell the stories of what took place in the natural world. What they looked like, sounded like, felt like to the touch. But the largest part of the experience, the greatest part of what is happening—the God part—is much more difficult to relate, because many times there is no explanation for it. Or perhaps a better way to say it is there is no explanation of it. God is the explanation for it, but the challenge is putting it into words. When you experience it, you understand. But when you haven't, it's easy to get bogged down and derailed by legalistic technicalities.

For example, I have a friend named Val. When she and I get together we frequently find ourselves on wonderful journeys into the supernatural realm. On one occasion we were in the kitchen at church, washing our hands and getting ready to walk out. All of a sudden the Holy Spirit came down thick, and at the same time we both hit the floor. Thankfully, it was a clean floor!

I had just been sharing with her that recently during my time with the Lord He had given me a new name. He had been taking me to areas of the Bible where He had given people new names, and I was fascinated by it. I had just recently asked Him if He had a new name for me, and He told me His name for me was Rose.

At first I thought *Rose? Why Rose? Roses aren't even my favorite flower.* I didn't understand. However, God gave me a vision of a beautiful white rose and said this was my name.

This grew to have a very special meaning for me, as I discovered that in the book of Isaiah there is a verse which declares that the desert shall bloom like the rose. I was reminded of the verse He had given me about new life springing up in the dry wilderness. I also later learned that white and red roses together serve as a special reminder of Jesus' crucifixion and resurrection.

But believe it or not, right there in the kitchen I had been telling Val my story…and Boom!

Next thing I knew we were on our knees, and laughing so hard we were doubled over. The joy in that place was so heavy, if that makes any sense. It was pressing us to the floor! We both crawled across the floor and were trying to get the door open, which was making us laugh even more. Finally, we made it out, and—still on our knees—crawled to a table and began trying to pull ourselves up into the chairs. Again, it was very difficult because this whoosh of joy, this heavy blanket, just kept covering us and would not let up. Finally, Val was able to pull herself into the chair, and as soon as she did she shouted out…"OH MY

GOSH! I GOT A NAME!"

Not even asking for it, Val had been given the name Pearl. She immediately began to cry, as God explained to her that He saw her as a Pearl because of all the difficulties she had endured, which ended up making her into the lovely person she is. It was such a special moment, and to this day we still refer to each other as Rose and Pearl.

Isn't that beautiful? And fun?

Several months after this experience, Val invited me to go to a small church that was meeting in a warehouse park. A friend of hers was preaching for one of his first times and she wanted to support him. When we got there, a group of about thirty people were gathered and worship was just starting. It quickly became evident that although this place was plain, and bare, the Holy Spirit was in the house!

As the four-person band played, I was standing on the concrete floor completely enjoying worship, having a wonderful time. Suddenly, I was just…not there. God took me to another place. It sounds wild, but I completely knew, without a doubt, I was at that other place. I knew in the natural I had never left the church…but it didn't change the reality of the fact that I was also gone. Both were equally real at the same time, and somehow they were not in conflict with each other.

I found myself on a sidewalk, in a light drizzle, standing in front of an old cobblestone building. It seemed to me like it might have been London, as there were old iron street lamps with high, rounded tops. Right then a lady came running out of the building carrying a baby wrapped up in a small blanket, and I heard the Lord say, *The baby will die unless you pray for his fever to go.*

She stopped right where I was standing, and I said, "Ma'am, the Lord has sent me to pray for your baby. May I pray for your baby?"

She didn't speak. She just nodded. I laid my hands on the baby's forehead, and said, "In the name of Jesus Christ, I command the fever to go."

Just then a car came around the corner, evidently driven by her husband. I sensed I had caught them rushing to the hospital, and I told her, "Go on to the hospital. Your baby will be fine."

I knew without a doubt that her baby was healed.

As soon as the car pulled away I found myself somewhere else. I was in a very plain and simple bedroom, standing next to a bed. There was an elderly lady lying in front of me, with her eyes closed, as if she was sleeping. God told me, *I brought you here because she did not want to die alone. I want you to be with her.*

I reached out, and I'm telling you this, as certain as I believe anything else I hold dear in my heart: I held her hand. I felt the frail bones underneath the loose skin. I sensed her fingers wrap slightly around mine. She did not open her eyes to look at me, but I knew that she knew I was there. I stayed for several minutes, and in that time I could sense the whole of her being starting to relax, and become at peace. Eventually, as I stood there and held her hand, I saw angels come into the room to get her, and I saw her spirit go with them. It was not dramatic; just a very smooth, easy happening.

And then I was back, standing in the little church in the middle of worship. I was almost in shock, thinking, *Did that just happen?* But I knew without a doubt it had. I wanted to turn and tell Val, but right then I couldn't even speak of it. It was too special, too holy. Even to this day, I regard it as one of the most precious gifts that God has given me, to allow me to be there in her final moments.

The fact I never left the church can never convince me I was not also at this woman's side during that time. If you were in the church, watching me, you would swear I was there the whole time. I never left. And in a strictly natural explanation, you would be right. But I also understand that the natural—what we see, what we hear, what we touch and taste—is only a small part of what is actually going on. The larger part of reality, the far greater percentage of all that exists, is taking place in the supernatural all around us at all times. And it is in this place where God desires to do amazing things through us, and it is to this place we must be willing to go, and just show up.

The fruit of our relationship with God will certainly appear in the natural. We will see the waves. People will be healed, lives will be restored, wondrous things will come to be. But we can't live only in the natural and expect all this to happen. We have to be willing to open ourselves up and let God have His way across the entire spectrum of His reality, not just the part that can be seen from the world's point of view.

That evening at this tiny church, Val's friend Jon spoke on healing. I had recently received some test results from a doctor that I was concerned about, and after the service when he asked for people to come up for prayer I went forward. Again, the Holy Spirit sent me to the floor. There was definitely healing going on in my body, that much was obvious. In fact, the next time they ran the test, the abnormalities I had been concerned about were gone.

As I write this, something else is becoming obvious: it seems like every time Val and I get together we end up on the floor, covered with the Holy Spirit. We should hang out more often!

Anyway, a few days later God prompted me to give Jon a call and thank him, so I reached out to Val and got his number. While I had Jon on the phone, God told me to tell him all the things that had been happening in my ministry lately. We ended up talking for quite a while, which was not unusual at this time. With all the new stuff I was experiencing, I loved to talk to other people in ministry about what God was doing in my life and find out what He was doing in theirs.

So we were having this great conversation about all these things, and I began to tell Jon about the deliverance I had experienced at Dee's house. I explained that it felt like a demon had just lifted off of me, physically, and I had never experienced anything like that before as long as I'd been a Christian.

Now I didn't know it at the time (Jon related this to me much later) but he had been going through a real challenge of his own lately. In his own ministry, God had been leading him to preach on deliverance more frequently, and it wasn't uncommon for people to come forward. As he watched more and more people being delivered, Jon began wrestling with the question of whether these people were actually saved or not. He was speaking in churches, to mainly what were assumed to be Christian audiences, so it made the whole thing all that much more puzzling to him.

In addition to that, on a separate issue, he had been dealing with a rage problem of his own. It was something that he could not control, whether it was toward his family members or other drivers in traffic, it would just come up and burst out, leaving him wondering where it even came from.

But unaware of all this at the time, I just went on with the conversation, telling Jon about how much I loved Jesus and oh, by the way, had recently felt a demon lift off of me. When I said this, he actually blurted out, "Do you think you can deliver me of the demon of rage?"

Jon says he knew it was the Holy Spirit because he did not intend to ask this question. It was completely unintentional. It wasn't on his mind, and it wasn't even a question he would have asked, because he knew he was saved. There was no reason for him to think that, as a Christian, he needed deliverance from any demons.

But I answered, "Of course. Let me ask God who He wants there and we'll get it set up."

It turned out to be Laurie, Val, and myself, about a week later, at a one room apartment that we sometimes used for ministry. When Jon and his wife arrived, God immediately highlighted her to me, and I knew I was to pray with her. She and I went over into the corner of the room and began to pray, while Laurie and Val began to pray with Jon on the couch.

Laurie began by asking why he was there, (taking full advantage of this no-preparation thing) and Jon replied, "Anger. I take it out on my kids, on my wife. I know how bad it is and I don't want to do it, but I do it anyway. It's like in the moment I have no control over what I do, and I always regret it later."

So she and Val began praying, and following the Holy Spirit's direction, went straight after the demon of rage. With Val praying in tongues, Laurie called forth the spirit of rage from within Jon. It went something like this: "Spirit of rage, in the name of Jesus Christ, I command you to come to the front!"

She had Jon confess that he had come into agreement with this spirit, and had him renounce in the name of Jesus any generational curses associated with it, and break agreement with the spirit of rage. At this time some really odd sounds started coming out of him and he lost the ability to talk. This went on for a few minutes, until he began shaking uncontrollably as Laurie kept repeating, many times, "Come out in the name of Jesus! Come out in the name of Jesus!"

Jon doesn't recall anything about what happened next, but he stiffened and fell over sideways on the sofa, letting out a scream that lasted several minutes. It was long enough and loud enough that I actually walked out into the street to make sure it wasn't drawing attention. The apartment was across the road from a fire hall, and I wanted to make sure these guys weren't heading over with their axes drawn!

Finally the spirit of rage left his body, and Jon went completely limp. At this time Laurie began to pray blessings of peace and calmness and patience and self-control over him. She began to speak the love of God into him, asking His love to fill all the empty places that were left behind when this demon of rage was cast out. Jon began to cry like a child, completely overcome by the love and peace and goodness of God.

And of course, when we looked over at Val, she was laid out on the floor. She had worn a dress, and was flat on her back, with her eyes closed, making grunting noises like, "Hurreh! Hut! Herrera!"

Laurie told me later she made a mental note to always wear pants when she does deliverance.

Now here's the point of me telling you all this: today, Jon has an incredible ministry, doing, of all things...deliverance! He has radically changed the lives of countless people, most of them Christians. He has helped them find freedom from the bondages of all sorts of ugliness and evil in their lives. His willingness to follow God through something that didn't make sense to him released his true gifting and calling, and has yielded fruit 100 times, 1000 times over. Today he travels the world with his ministry.

This is not the only time I have seen where a firmly-held belief, or an irrational fear, or something along those lines stands directly in the way of God's calling on a person's life. If Satan knows your true calling is to have a ministry providing medical flights to underprivileged countries, it wouldn't surprise me to learn at one time you had a deathly fear of flying. If your true calling is a deliverance ministry, he might give you a firm conviction that "this deliverance stuff is really not for Christians."

Remember, the battle is in the mind. The enemy will attack you in your mind with a lie, wherever he thinks he can keep you from producing fruit. But our God is a great and mighty God, able to tear down strongholds and cause all darkness to flee. The truth of who God is cancels out every one of Satan's lies, and that truth, that power, is alive in the heart of every single believer, waiting to do battle.

Jon tells me that to this day, he has never again been attacked by that uncontrollable rage.

CHAPTER 14

WHO WILL GIVE THEM A HOME?

───────── ❧ ─────────

Never let the natural limit the supernatural.

Whether it's a lie, or a mental roadblock, or even your circumstances. These things are no problem for God, but it is up to us to choose to believe He can handle them, rather than choosing to believe they are insurmountable. It's amazing the power we have to either win a Kingdom battle or lose a Kingdom battle simply based on what we choose to believe.

While all the things I'm telling you about in this book took place, the real estate market crashed, taking the entire US economy and a lot of people down with it. My husband and I both had jobs associated with real estate and construction, and quickly found ourselves in a very bad spot. Seemingly overnight our income was gone, and there was no obvious way to replace it any time soon. It was a very strange time, and we ended up losing not only jobs, but also savings, cars, and finally even our home.

There was a season where we knew our house was gone, but we still lived in it. In this same season Laurie and her family were also in the process of losing their home. Things were looking pretty dark, and neither of us had the financial means at hand to do anything about it. But thankfully these circumstances existed only in the natural realm. God is not confined to the natural, and when we join Him in the supernatural, neither are we!

During this time of not knowing where our families would live the next month, Laurie and her friend came over and asked if we could pray about a certain house in the area. On the way to our church, along a road that was somewhat out in the country, there was this magnificent house for sale. It had a huge block wall along the road with an iron gate, and you could look through the gate and see the house and the grounds inside. The house itself, believe it or not, was almost Barbie doll pink…but it worked because it was styled as if it was from the Victorian era. It had large columns, and tall doors and windows, and sat at the end of a winding brick drive in the middle of acres of oak trees covered with spanish moss.

Laurie had been sensing such a supernatural draw to this house that many times she had to just pull over and stop, and pray in front of it. It made no logical sense, because she was in no position to buy a house, and wouldn't choose this one even if she were. The purchase price was way more money than she would ever likely spend on a house. And yet, God kept highlighting this place every time she drove past. There was definitely something He had on His mind, and He kept placing it on hers. She simply couldn't let it go.

When they came over that day before church and told me about it, I'll admit the thought crossed my mind: Wow! A huge pink house! And here we are, losing our home, and Laurie's losing her home, and it's so big we could both move in…and I guess we could paint it, maybe…

But the whole thing made no sense. Neither of our families had any money, and both of our husbands' work situations were shaky at best during this time. Nevertheless, here was an opportunity to pray, so the three of us prayed. It's what we did. It's who we were, and it's how we were operating these days… we were the crazy ladies that pray, and sure enough we prayed about everything!

So when we got started praying about this house…WOW! We knew immediately that we had stepped into the middle of a HUGE battle taking place in the supernatural. There was so much warfare going on it was incredible. What I mean is this: sometimes in prayer we would go to a real gentle place, and we would rest back in our seats and our tongues would be soft, and flowing…and sometimes, like now, our tongues would become strong, and fierce. We would get to our feet and even act like we were drawing swords. We would turn, and point, and declare things in the supernatural we didn't even know the meaning of. God would tell us, *Claim this land!* and we would drive our invisible stake into the earth and claim that ground for the Kingdom.

One of the most beautiful, most unexpected, most rewarding things about being able to hear the supernatural is the ability to discern where the real battles are. Some things which appear calm in the natural world are actually major focal points of spiritual warfare. Imagine for a second the spiritual warfare taking place around Jesus as a new baby: to the neighbors, it probably seemed like no big deal, Joseph and Mary have a new kid, and He never seems to get in trouble…but in the spiritual world, Satan was trying everything he could to make sure that Jesus did not grow into the fullness of His ministry. I'll bet the warring angels protecting our Lord had their hands full, every day!

Well, whatever was happening around this pink house, it was

intense! We battled for almost two hours, and I'm sure if someone had filmed it we could have sold it for a workout video. But by this time in our adventures we had come to know two things: one, this fierce, forceful prayer somehow made a difference in the supernatural Kingdom...it mattered to God; and two, if there was this much of a battle going on in the spiritual realm, something big must be at stake.

So that day in my humble living room, we had stepped right into the middle of a battle over spiritual territory. One which would have a generational impact on the Kingdom of God. We came out of that prayer session declaring to the Lord we would say *Yes,* no matter what He asked us in reference to this pink house.

It was time to head to church, and Laurie and I jumped in my car and took off with her friend following. Of course, this took us right by the house, so we stopped in the driveway to get the information from the "For Sale" sign. We had agreed we should call and set up an appointment to see the house, and while we were there we again took the opportunity to pray.

Because we always prayed. It's what we did.

Back in the car, on the way to church, God revealed something to me, so clear, so strong. I turned to Laurie and said, "God just told me we are supposed to start a home for human trafficking survivors."

Tears immediately filled Laurie's eyes. "Oh my gosh, that makes so much sense..."

Just weeks before, right about the time God began placing this pink house on Laurie's heart, she had gone to an event and watched a video about the horrors of human trafficking. It focused on a survivor who had been rescued from trafficking, who at the end had asked the question, "Where do I go now that

I'm finally out? I can't go back where I came from before this all happened, because I'm not the same person...But where do I go?"

The video faded to the words on the screen, "Who will give them a home?"

Laurie's heart had been struck with a pain that was not normal, not to be ignored. She had known without a doubt it was God, and she remembered crying out to Him in her Spirit, *God, somebody needs to do something! Somebody needs to give them a home!*

When we arrived at church and parked, I was excited, and hurried over to the other car. "I know what the pink house is all about!"

"So do I," her friend said, stepping out.

I stopped short. "Really? What?"

"God wants to start a home for human trafficking survivors. He just showed me on the way here."

After church, back at my house, I actually had to google human trafficking. I wasn't really sure what it was, but I was absolutely certain God had said we needed to start a home for the survivors.

The next weekend the listing agent met us at the big pink house and let us in. Since I had an active realtor's license, she opened the house and left, instructing us to lock up on the way out. As we made our way around the house and the property, praying, we were continually in awe of the magnificence that confronted us at every turn. Everything was taller, and grander, and more ornate than we expected after only glimpsing the house from the street. In the back yard was a beautiful open courtyard with a huge pool, with another entire house on the other side.

The property was large and lush, and surrounded by a wall in front and a privacy fence on all sides. It gave us a great sense of security while at the same time providing the peacefulness of open, natural space. It was very easy to see how this would be the perfect environment for someone to pause, and rest, and heal, and gather their life back together.

As we did a final round to make sure everything was locked up before leaving, we were overwhelmed by a sense of so much pain, so much loss, so much…darkness. I knew that God was revealing His heart, and sharing the depth of the pain He felt over this horrible injustice that was happening to the ones He loved so desperately. Of course at this time I did not know that this would be the type of home that God would give us later on for human trafficking survivors. In other words, He was showing us what was to come.

CHAPTER 15

BECAUSE OTHERS WON'T

————————~❧~————————

According to Hebrews 11:1, faith is the substance of things hoped for, the evidence of things not seen.

When you have been given a seed, and you have put it in the dirt, there is a season when outward appearances are deceiving. Even though you appear to be empty-handed, you know that you have something very valuable...you have a promise. You carry, and hold on to, the substance of things hoped for.

Since we knew God had definitely revealed we were to help human trafficking survivors, we took this very seriously. We began to do everything we could think of that aligned with His plans. We contacted every organization we could find that was involved with human trafficking, and did very in-depth research on them, even traveling great distances to meet with a number of them. We wanted to know what they were doing, exactly, and how they were doing it. We wanted to know what worked, and what failed, and why. There was also a trip to the other end of the state, to meet the owners of the pink house and relate what God had told us, on the off chance that they might give us this magnificent piece of property.

They didn't. But you never know, right? He's a big God...

We subscribed to everything, read everything, attended everything that had anything to do with human trafficking. We told everyone we came across what God's plans were, what He had revealed to us. We let them know that the crazy ladies that prayed were starting a home for human trafficking survivors, on direct revelation from God. Because of the work we did, the seriousness we put into the research and the contacts, we were quickly becoming experts on the subject of human trafficking.

But still...God had promised a home. That was the seed we knew was buried in the dirt, and that thing was not breaking the earth no matter how much Holy Spirit water we poured on it. We were supposed to give them a home, and we didn't have one. Shoot, we didn't even have our own by this time.

And I'm sure to some people, to use a country expression, it might have seemed like these crazy ladies that pray were "All hat, no cattle." In fact when people referred to us, some of them emphasized *pray*...and some of them emphasized *crazy*.

But that was okay, because we had heard our God. He had revealed this to us when we didn't even really know what it was, and confirmed it in a way only He could. God had personally invited us to join Him in a major spiritual battle that deeply touched His heart, and it was something that mattered to Him.

So it mattered to us.

One time we were at a conference for human trafficking, and after learning in-depth the details of what human trafficking survivors go through, meeting them in person, hearing their personal stories, and watching the horrific videos, I honestly felt like I couldn't take it anymore. I went back to the hotel room, completely overwhelmed, and dropped onto the bed.

Oh, God, I said, *Are you sure this is where you want me? It feels like it's too hard.*

God said, *Yes, Misty. This is exactly where I want you.*

But...why did you choose me?

Because others won't.

Ouch...

Oh, Father...thank you. Thank you, for allowing me.

In the meantime people were calling us left and right to pray with them, about every situation under the sun. Inner healing, deliverance, physical pain, it didn't matter. People had told people about their experiences and our phones would not stop ringing. We just kept asking God who should go help these people, then we'd get prayed up and show up. The rest we left up to Him, and He never...I mean never...failed to do something amazing. It's easy when you're not in control, and you have a leader like God!

One of the most wonderful things about living in the Spirit, moving in the Spirit, making every move based on the Holy Spirit, is looking back and seeing how things actually lined up and came together. How God was setting you up behind the scenes when you didn't even realize it was happening. Over time, things which seemed like little coincidences, disconnected happenings in life, actually came together and began to lay out as the stepping stones of His larger plan.

I began to recognize, even before I was baptized in the Spirit and began this journey, things that happened during my day and week that would make me go, *Hmm... That was cool how that worked out.* And while I'm certainly not saying that every coincidence is a move of God, I can say that many I thought to be coincidence proved later to be God connections.

As an example, during the time that Laurie and I were receiving the baptism of the Holy Spirit in Florida, a lady named Elizabeth was experiencing her own radical baptism in Chicago. And it was no coincidence that her family was planning a move to Florida in the near future.

I marvel at the wisdom of God, when He gave Adam the job of tending the garden. As I mentioned earlier, a seed can sit in the ground for quite a while before we notice anything at all happening. Gardening requires faith and determination to do our part, even when there is no fruit, and it requires a belief in the promise of God that He will bring His promises to pass.

And after many months of watering what seemed to be empty dirt...the seed finally broke the earth.

Dee called, and said there was a lady named Elizabeth in town who had heard about Laurie and I, and wanted to meet us. She was new in the area, and told Dee that she had been involved with a Holy Spirit-filled group of prayer warriors back in Chicago, and wanted to meet the same kind of people here.

I told Dee that I would love to get together, but right now I was so busy that I truly don't have the time. I let her know that I would get back in touch when things took a break.

Of course things never took a break, and about a month or so later Dee called back, and said that Elizabeth was organizing a

Spiritual Spa, a weekend gathering for women leaders from the surrounding areas, and had asked if Laurie and I wanted to be intercessors for the event. And of course I knew I was too busy, and I knew this wasn't what God had in His plans for me right now, but like everything else I told her I would pray about it.

So I hung up the phone, and I asked God about it...and He came back with an absolute *Yes!*

Of course when I volunteered myself that also meant Laurie, so the two of us got together and met with a group of women about the upcoming event. The discussions were mainly about the need for a common cause, a rallying point that the whole weekend could revolve around. They needed some local charity that they could raise awareness and support for.

And then Elizabeth said the most amazing thing: "Do you know I just learned that this area, Sarasota, has been identified as a major hub for human trafficking? Do you realize that our kids are being sold for sex, right here in our own back yard?"

God had set us up.

All three of us. He had placed it on Laurie's heart, brought it to Elizabeth's mind, and revealed it to my Spirit. He was beginning to form a partnership that He would use to bind this horrible offense that was taking place in His Kingdom. He had brought three Holy Spirit-filled women together so they could strengthen each other, and do more than one or two of them could ever do alone.

It's amazing when we think about it: Elizabeth enjoyed the business side, Laurie has a Mom's heart and loves to nurture, and I am all about the Holy Spirit, and sold out to following His direction no matter where it takes me.

We met shortly after and spent an entire weekend in prayer,

exploring the width and depth of exactly what God was thinking when He brought us together. He revealed an incredible blueprint: we would have multiple homes, and there would be two organizations, one as an umbrella for the other. The level of detail that God revealed was astonishing...he had evidently been thinking about this for quite some time.

We were on our knees one weekend asking God for the name of the organization. I heard the word "Selah." I knew that the word was used at the ending of verses in Psalms but I wasn't sure exactly what it meant. We looked up the word to find the meaning: to pause, reflect, and note the connection of precious truths.

We knew we had our name: Selah Freedom.

So the Spiritual Spa weekend finally took place, and human trafficking was highlighted as the cause everyone could rally around. And rally they did! Selah Freedom was presented as the premier local ministry working to not only fight against the spread of human trafficking, but also provide help and assistance to those rescued out of it.

The ministry launched with force. From a hazy vision given to women on their knees in the living room of a repossessed home, it grew into a full operating ministry that actually owned multiple homes in a crazy short period of time. Beginning with a rental home in downtown Sarasota, within four years there were several homes in multiple states. One of them was even very similar in style to the pink house which we originally visited.

We established an entire portion of the ministry specifically to work with local law enforcement and judges, training them to spot evidence of trafficking and offering them tools and resources to utilize when they did. We established a solid lobbying entity at the governmental level, and were successful in authoring and enacting Florida's first-ever law specifically targeted at human trafficking. An entire curriculum was created for the schools, and a separate group of people were solely focused on providing educational services into the K-12 school systems.

And of course, we began to house, feed, and care for many, many women who had been rescued out of the horrible life that is human trafficking. The ministry provided a loving, fulfilling, restful live-in environment where they could step out of their past and begin the process of healing and rebuilding their future. We offered completely free support, for as long as they needed, all the way through earning their GED, going on to college, and establishing a career.

The need turned out to be so great, and the support so strong, that the organization took off like a rocket. It was amazing to stand back and witness what God had planned...and what He did through everyday people who decided to just show up, and turn everything over to His direction.

The three of us prayed about every single step, all along the way. Big decisions, small decisions, decisions that seemed like no-brainers...everything was brought before God, and many times what He told us to do was way outside of what normal thinking would have been.

But of course that only makes sense. Following the world's normal thinking would have resulted in a normal path of growth, over a normal period of time. But God has a way of side-stepping things...miracle multiplication, turning water to wine, that kind of stuff. We were constantly in awe of the fruit coming from His ministry, and there was absolutely no way we could look at any of it and even begin to take credit.

The birth and incredible rapid growth of Selah Freedom was all due to God, and God alone.

CHAPTER 16

SHUTTING DOWN

———— ✌ ————

As awesome as it was to see the ministry growing, I was questioning the direction God had me moving in personally. While Laurie and Elizabeth seemed to have ready-made spots within the Selah organization, God continued to tell me I was not supposed to be on staff. He was very clear about it, and no matter how many times I asked Him He would say, *Trust me. You are supposed to be separate.*

During this season a local pastor's wife returned from a mission trip overseas. While in Africa, God had given her a vision of a prayer house that she should establish at her church. This was to be a free, open place where people could come and be touched by God in whatever way they needed. When she got back and began to pray about who would head up this new prayer house, she felt like God highlighted me.

Now, one thing I was sure of in my life at this time: I did not have a single minute to do anything additional to what I was already doing. I was running 24/7, stretched to the limit with things that God was bringing to my plate. Just to make it clear, I didn't have hobbies. I didn't do knitting on Tuesdays and tennis on Wednesdays and chorus on Thursdays. (If you've ever heard me sing, you know why I didn't do chorus on Thursdays.)

What I did was God. I did God every day. Every day I was somewhere, with somebody, praying for something. My first thought when this lady called me was, *Well, I believe that's what God told you, but I don't think that's what He's going to tell me.*

But I prayed anyway, and sure enough, God said, *Do it.*

Now I was really confused. There were only so many hours in the day. I was certain God had called me to help start Selah Freedom, and it seemed like it was finally getting rolling. It was gaining some legs! I also knew that God was calling me to the prayer ministry. Time and time and time again He would show me, by His fruit, I was hearing His voice, heeding His call, and on the right path. And now, when I didn't have a spare moment in the day, He wanted me to start a prayer house.

A prayer house? I thought I was supposed to be a part of this survivor house? And just a reminder, God...I still need my own house!

The whole thing just didn't seem to fit, and I could very easily have not done it. But at this point in my life, I was sold out, and completely accustomed to following directions that didn't make sense. Besides, this one sort of did, because after all it was a prayer house. It wasn't that crazy of a thing for Him to ask me to do, like start a flying school or something. It just truly seemed like I didn't have time. It would be a full-time, completely volunteer position. I would be running the complete organization, and managing an entire staff of volunteers, both things I had no experience at. But I got prayed up, and I jumped in head-first.

The Prayer House was the first place I was really forced to think about the amazing things God had been doing in my life, and figure out how to effectively teach these things to other people. We pulled curriculums from trusted ministries, and I added in additional material as the Holy Spirit led me in order to teach a group of dedicated volunteers how to effectively reach people through powerful prayer. We wanted to engage people in a way that made a difference in their lives, whether it was through healing, deliverance, cancellation of generational curses, tearing down enemy strongholds, or whatever else God revealed.

We were after radical transformation in people's lives. We wanted the broken and lost people that came to our house to leave there completely saved, completely healed, and completely restored. We wanted them to have a true encounter with God's love, power, and grace, and to develop a close, personal relationship with Him.

And it was a huge success. We had several dozen volunteers and served hundreds and hundreds of people. Not only did we provide freedom sessions to the community, we also provided training to other organizations that wanted to start a Prayer House in their area as well. At one point Heidi Baker's school of ministry came into town. We connected with them and had the opportunity to teach her students everything we were learning.

I grew in obvious ways from seeing God work in so many different situations, but also in subtle ways, such as becoming better at leading a team of people.

So now Breathe Freedom Ministries was blossoming all over. I was at the Prayer House most days, and when I wasn't I put on my co-founder hat for Selah Freedom. Laurie, Elizabeth, and I were together constantly in the evenings and weekends, praying through every decision: who should be on the board of directors, who should be hired and in what role, what color the carpet in the newest house should be.

It was a good season. I was able to go into Selah Freedom and work with the girls, worship with them, share the love and grace of Jesus Christ, and the power of the Holy Spirit. We baptized them in swimming pools, bathtubs, the Gulf of Mexico... wherever we could. I also continued to go into the Prayer House and the community, ministering to people in their homes, in the streets, in food pantries...anywhere God wanted me to go. All along, though, God continued to show me, very clearly, *Selah Freedom over there...and Breathe Freedom Ministries over here.* There was never a doubt that the two ministries were separate in His eyes, and I came to know in my heart that it was His design for Breathe Freedom to eventually step into bigger things.

With Breathe Freedom Ministries starting to expand, I knew I only had so many hours in a day. So, two years after starting the Prayer House, there came a season when I knew it was time to hand over the reins. I stepped aside from my position and allowed others to rise up and grow into the fullness of what God had for them.

God was on the move. His Kingdom was advancing. My ministry was no longer going to be confined to just one neighborhood, or even one town like the Prayer House was. God was wanting me to serve more people, on a broader scale. It was at this time that I knew Breathe Freedom Ministries should become a 501(c)3. This would allow the ministry to expand wherever, whenever, and however the Lord wanted.

Both the Prayer House and Selah Freedom certainly qualified as God doing a new thing. They were each providing ways in the wilderness, and streams of Living Water in the wasteland. They were obviously ministries that were close to God's heart, as He showed up time and time again, through miracle after miracle. I am so blessed He allowed me to be a part of each of them, but I was beginning to feel in my spirit that there were some changes coming…He wasn't finished yet.

About this time, I went on a trip for my birthday. The day after I returned I knew I was sick. Everyone had this cough/fever thing that was going around, so I just assumed I was next. I waited for it to move on, but after about ten days I started thinking a doctor visit might be in order. The first visit, they checked for all the usuals, flu, strep, etc. All the tests came back negative and normal, except my kidney function was a little off. They advised me to stop taking so much night-time cold medication because it could affect the kidneys.

A few more weeks went by. The cough went away but I still had a low-grade fever. I went to a different doctor, and ended up with more tests, more normal results. We added in antibiotics, because even though they weren't finding anything, something was wrong. A few more weeks passed, and I still had a low-grade fever and was starting to sleep a large portion of the day. Lung x-rays told me I had spots on my lungs, so now they thought it might be cancer. I had further tests, but that turned out to be nothing. So they switched antibiotics, and threw in some steroids. A few weeks later I still had a low-grade fever and now my eye was starting to hurt. A different doctor gave me pink-eye medication, and more antibiotics, and scheduled a CAT scan.

This went on for over two months.

By this time I could barely function. I was starting to call

all my prayer warrior friends, and tell them we were way past regular prayer...I was asking for warfare prayer. While I was waiting for the results of the CAT scan to come back, I had a choice: there was a business trip I had planned for four months with Selah Freedom, and I really wanted to go and complete some things that I had started. I begged the doctor to allow me to go; after all, it was only a few days and we would have the CAT scan results by the time I got back.

Well, evidently I was pretty persuasive, because I boarded the plane wearing an eye patch and a mask (this was before the days of Covid). But once I got to Texas, it became very clear... things were not okay.

I remember lying in the hotel bed thinking, *What am I doing? I never should have even considered taking this trip. This thing is bigger than I thought.* The whole time at the hotel, I couldn't get out of bed. The doctor called, and said the CAT scan showed infection in my kidneys and I needed to come in so they could treat it. *Okay*, I thought, *there's something*. That didn't seem too bad...until I started throwing up each time I ate, and finally realized I couldn't eat at all.

At this point I knew I needed medical help, but I didn't want to go to a hospital in Texas. I wanted to wait until I got home. And I was getting scared. Really scared. I had done all I could do. I had prayed all I could pray, but I was not getting any clear answers from the Lord. After flying home late that night, my husband picked me up at the airport and I told him just to get me straight to bed.

The next morning, things went from bad to worse. When I woke up my husband had already left for work, and I realized my body was shutting down. I don't know how to explain it or describe it, except I just knew. Right at that moment, my friend Traci called, and told me God woke her up in the middle of the night several times to tell her to call me first thing in the morning. "Misty," she asked, "What in the world is going on?"

"My body is shutting down. I need to get to the Emergency Room."

"I'm already on the way," she said. "We're going right now... God told me it was IMPORTANT! Which one do you want to go to?"

Hmmm...I hadn't thought about this, so I went to my default answer. "I'm not sure. Let's pray and ask."

It is such a blessing to hear God speak in times when your brain is so overwhelmed that it can't possibly think straight. And even though I wasn't certain, God was: He wanted me to go to a hospital fifty miles away! Seriously? There were three right around the corner! And I would pass two more on the way there!

But if I didn't want His input I shouldn't have asked, right? So Traci showed up and away we went...

In the ER, they ran some quick tests with even quicker results: I was anemic, dehydrated, and my kidney function was less than 30%. I kept my face covered, because it was incredibly painful when any type of light touched my eyes. They immediately admitted me and placed me in a negative-pressure isolation room, where the staff could not even come in without wearing head-to-toe gear. I got tested for everything, and I mean everything. And just like before, every last test result came back negative, across the board.

On day two, after they were able to rule out the BIG stuff, a brave doctor walked in. I say "brave" because the first thing I noticed was he was not wearing an astronaut suit. He stood directly in front of me, and proclaimed, "This is absolute nonsense. I don't know what you have, but it's not contagious.

And I promise you I will find out…I'm bringing in everybody I can to find out what's going on here."

So about one full day and seven confused specialists later, a kind, soft-spoken doctor came into my room. He gently smiled and sat down in a chair beside my bed. He told me to call him Dr. B, because I had no chance at pronouncing his last name correctly. He had been looking over my files, and asked if I could please go over with him all that had happened to me in the past two months, from the moment I got sick until today in the hospital. He told me not to leave any details out, and he would just sit there and listen.

Well, okay. This was something I wasn't expecting, and very refreshing. So I got started, and we went through the early pains, and the later pains, and the first and second and third rounds of testing, and all the doctors, and all the guesses, and all the misses, and all the medications.

At the end of the story, he looked at me and said, "Misty, I think I know what is wrong."

"What? Really?"

"I think you have an autoimmune disease that is extremely rare…in fact, there have only been 250 confirmed cases in the world."

I was shocked. "How do you know? What clue did I give you?"

"It was the steroids—you said that at one point they had put you on steroids, and the fever went away for a few days…but when you went off, the temperature came right back."

At this point it did feel amazing to finally have an answer. I have always been a firm believer that the truth will set us free. But right behind the excitement came all kinds of other emotions, and a slew of questions, of course ending with, "What does this mean?"

"I'll need to do a kidney biopsy to confirm it, so I'll get that scheduled."

"Have you ever diagnosed anyone else with this? Have you ever seen anyone with this?"

"Oh, no…it is way too rare. It's mainly on the other side of the world."

I was thinking this man was truly sent to me by God! And then I remembered…I was sent to him, fifty miles away from home when I asked God which hospital I should go to, and heard Him answer with one that was not even on my mind.

"So tell me," I asked, "how did you even think about this? If it's so rare, how did you know?"

He smiled a gentle smile as he got up to leave. "It's my job to know. I'm a specialist, and I study all the rare diseases I can find. Just in case one ever comes my way."

Wow, God.

I knew right then I would be okay.

CHAPTER 17

THE MOST VALUABLE THING

Sure enough the biopsy came back positive, so I officially became case #251. There was no time to question how I ended up with something so rare, and so bizarre. Right now there was healing to be done!

I wasn't contagious, which meant I could hug my husband, and have some friends by, although my room continued to be pitch black. I even had blankets over the window, because my eyes couldn't handle any light whatsoever. The smallest amount of light on my eyes created a stabbing pain. They were so sensitive that even noise hurt…I could actually feel sound waves banging against my eyes! I learned that this disease initially attacked the kidneys and the eyes, eventually spreading to the other organs. My symptoms certainly backed that up. My eyes and kidneys were both barely functioning. To this day I'm still so grateful that God guided me to the one hospital where Dr. B was able to diagnose this disease before it went much further.

Ten days later I was finally released to go home. I was on 60mg of steroids every day, which is a ridiculous amount. I continued in heavy prayer, speaking healing over my kidneys, my eyes, and my immune system. Speaking God's truth over my health and my future. Taking the time to remind Him of each and every single promise He had made to me over the years, which had not yet come to be...and there were a lot!

It was a very difficult time. Every inch of my body hurt, all the way down inside my bones. In addition, I couldn't sleep, and my brain was having a tough time processing even the simplest things. God must have known I needed some good news, because a little bit came almost immediately.

The doctors had said that it would take about a year or two for my kidneys to recover completely, IF they ever did. Well...they were back to 100% within the first month! This filled me with hope, and reminded me that God was in the miracle business! I had spent the time in the hospital declaring His promises and speaking life and complete healing into my body, so you can imagine the victory I felt when my sweet Dr. B showed me the test results. It was an incredible celebration. *Okay,* I thought, *we're on the right track. One miracle down, and a few more to go!*

Even though my kidneys were better, the rest of me was a wreck. I spent a lot of the first few months just trying to survive, stay close to God, and get well. The whole situation was still so confusing it made my head hurt to think about it, literally. *Where had this come from? When would it be over?* My processing during this time was non-existent. I couldn't keep my brain on track long enough to finish a sentence, much less put two sentences together coherently. So most of the time I simply chose to not even try and think.

But for all the things I didn't remember, I did remember this: I had a healing ministry! I understood the spiritual battle I was called to fight against sickness and disease, and had a firm grasp on the weapons I could employ against it. I knew in my very spirit that my Father loved me and wanted me healed... completely! In other words, I knew I should not be this sick!

I mean, it's not like my faith in healing was the size of a mustard seed...it was an oak tree! It was big, and strong, and solid. I understood this stuff! I was called to it, and I lived it... so what was going on here? Why wasn't I healed? The anger and frustration of even trying to consider these things would completely exhaust me, until all I could do was lean on God, and rest. Not question. Not struggle. Just rest, and wait.

Eventually, even though my immune system was very weak, I took a trip to Tennessee to visit my sister. I remember the doctor had just given me a new report about my eyes, and he was very concerned about the muscles and blood vessels. In addition, the trip was causing a brand new level of aching in my bones that had not been there before. The Lord led us to a little country church that my sister and her husband were going to in the Smokey Mountains called Truth Church. (Love that name!) There was such a pure love in the air I could feel it when I walked through the doors.

The pastor of the church and his wife, in the middle of praise and worship, laid hands on me and prayed, and the aching in my bones went away immediately! Not gradually, but right there on the spot! It was the most incredible feeling. I just couldn't believe the difference. I had come into that service slow and in pain, but I walked out with a new skip in my step. It was amazing. In addition, when I got back from Tennessee and went for additional tests on my eyes, I wasn't surprised when the report came back favorable. Other things were still happening with my eyes, but the muscles and blood vessels were no longer a concern.

It was a rollercoaster of emotions during this time. I was happy with any progress, but at the same time frustrated by the fact that the disease had come all at once, like a freight train…but seemed to be leaving one boxcar at a time. God was obviously still working miracles, for which I was incredibly grateful, but that one all-encompassing complete recovery still hadn't come. For example, even though the eye doctor's immediate concern was gone, there were still other issues that need to be addressed. The autoimmune disease marched on, still active, still attacking… and I just didn't have an answer for it.

I was far from well, and the months dragged on. I read book after book, and repented for anything and everything I could. I looked for any open doors and closed all I could find. I praised God and cried out to God. I was so grateful for my friends during this time. They prayed with me non-stop, around the clock. In fact, I had entire ministries praying for me, some I didn't even know and will probably never meet. But I was truly blessed by the outpouring of love, and equally blessed by the many things I learned during this season. If nothing else, sitting on the receiving end this time, it was reinforced to me that healing is not a formula. It is not a system. The greatest thing we can do to help others when they are sick is to pray and just be available for them with whatever they need.

Since my medications were keeping my immune system weakened, many times my friends opted to not come by to visit. They would just call, and sit with me on the phone and pray. We would go up into the spiritual realm before the throne of God, which allowed me to set my issues to the side and focus on the Father. From there I could ask Him what my next step was, and which areas I needed to work on for healing.

Sometimes the answer was about loving my body, sometimes it was about loving other things about myself…and sometimes it was about just resting in Him, and allowing Him to do whatever He needed to do, whether He explained it or not. It was beautiful, and I'm so grateful for my friends that took the time to be there for me, and stand with me, and allow their presence and God's presence to heal.

They would call, without an agenda or a plan. They would just show up. They called simply to love me, and be with me in a loving gentle way. Their only goal was to help me find what God had to say for me for that day, that moment. They were the two or more that were gathered together with me in prayer, and it brought the power of God's presence in a way that helped me find clarity.

Some days the pain and the emotions and everything else would make it difficult for me to hear God, or sense His sweet presence, but when a beautiful friend would come along beside me and join me in prayer, peace and calm would eventually come. Clarity would unfold, and I would be able to spend some precious time with my Lord. So again, thank you to all of you who were a part of that.

At around six months I had checkup appointments with a few of my doctors. When I visited the first one, she looked at my latest test results and gave me a whole new wave of things to be discouraged about: I was obese, I had extremely high cholesterol, and I had high liver levels from the autoimmune disease. She told me that I had three months to lose weight and work on the levels, and if I didn't make changes she was going to put me on all kinds of additional medications.

Right after that, while visiting a different specialist, I was given the news that I had to remain on my current meds for up to year. And for good measure, almost as an afterthought, she threw in, "You're going to gain a bunch of weight on these steroids, and experience a lot of side effects."

I knew she was just doing her job and trying to prepare me, but as soon as I walked out of her office and got in my car, I rebuked every word she had spoken! I let the spiritual realm know right then and there that I absolutely did not come into agreement with anything she declared over me! Instead, I continued to speak perfect health over my body, out loud, and proclaim that I was not going to gain weight...in fact, I was going to lose weight! And I was going to get healthy, in fact healthier than I had ever been, and have complete healing in Jesus' name!

But when all the rebuking and proclaiming victory was done...I just wanted to cry.

When I was in the hospital, fighting for my life, I realized for the first time in my life just how valuable my health was. In fact, it wasn't just important, it was the MOST valuable thing that I had. It didn't matter how much money I had, or who I knew, or what I had accomplished in life. Without my health I had nothing, I had no future. I wouldn't get to see my son get married, or my daughter have our first grandchild!

Without good health, everything would suffer: the destiny my ministry was called to fulfill, all the travel I should have done, all the time I should have spent holding grand babies. When health was gone, no amount of money in the world would buy it back. I began to realize it was a precious, precious, gift... and I could feel it slipping away.

Jesus tells us to take care of our bodies, that our bodies are the temple of the Holy Spirit. It states this so many times in His Word. Even though I had previously read and known this, I never understood the magnitude of the importance until I was ill.

Fighting for my life opened my eyes to the preciousness of

every moment of every day. There was a new appreciation for my temple, and I was ready to bring it some freedom. I was ready to fight for my future. Things really began to come into crystal-clear focus. I had bondage in my body, and I needed freedom. There was only one way to do that: complete surrender. Surrendering to the point of allowing God to fillet me wide open.

I began to tell God, right then, that I was serious. I needed His guidance. I didn't want to live like this...I needed my health restored! I needed my life back! I reminded Him of the plans He had for me, and the promises He had made me. I had a lot of Kingdom work to do and needed to get it done!

I began to speak over my future, and claim it for His glory. I refused to be in bondage with my body anymore. I told God I was completely surrendered to whatever He wanted me to do. I wanted my health and my future back. Whatever He wanted, I would do.

And like so many times in the past, the first real step to major change was getting desperate.

Within a very short time, my friend Thristene came to my house for a Bible study I had started in my home. While she was there, she told me about a health program that a lot of her friends were on, and that they'd been successful losing weight and getting healthy. She said she was ready to develop a healthy lifestyle that was sustainable. Well, the Holy Spirit began leaping inside me as she spoke...and I was all ears! I didn't even know what program she was talking about, but God was already confirming that this was it! He was bringing me a solution and this would be the program that would bring healing to my body. This was exactly what I had been crying out for! I told Thristene, "I don't have to hear any more. Sign me up. I don't care what it is, but I know it's my answer to prayer."

Thristene and I both signed up right away and started our journey together. Immediately, I started seeing results and feeling better. Finally, miraculously, I was able to deal with the extra weight I had been carrying for so many years. After only two months, I walked back into my primary doctor's office (the one who was going to put me on all the medications) and she was shocked. Not only had I dropped a ton of weight, but my cholesterol and my liver levels were back to normal, and all inflammation had left my body. Over the next five months I continued to lose, dropping a total of seventy-five pounds! *Thank you Jesus!*

The effects of this were amazing, not only for my body but for my mental and emotional state as well. I found confidence I didn't even know I lacked. I discovered energy that the sickness had completely stolen, and even my processing started to return. I could think again! I hadn't felt so stinking good since I was a teenager.

My body continued to heal at an incredible pace, finally even leading to a wonderful report about my eyes...I remember my doctor smiling as he told me that there was some scar tissue, but the eyes themselves were better than he had ever seen them, and should be good for a long time to come.

And to this day, many years later, I still feel fantastic! The doctors say the disease is in remission...but I say I'm healed!

God wants His people well. It's heavy on His heart.

I know this because He talks with me about it all the time. He has told me to pay this gift forward by helping as many people as I can. Through my testimony, I am able to let others know there is hope and a solution. He wants His people healthy so they can live the life they were created to live. He wants them to live victoriously!

Years ago during prayer, when I was still working with Selah Freedom, God specifically told me: "People die from lack of knowledge of my Word, and they die from lack of knowledge of nutrition. I want you to go and spread nutrition like you do my Word."

At the time I thought *That's crazy God, I don't even understand nutrition!*

Now, years later, I totally get it. Never before in history have people been in such bondage with their physical bodies, and I was no exception. Before my illness, I remember walking into the grocery store and feeling incredibly frustrated because I wanted to eat well, but truly didn't know what to buy. Every time I turned around there was conflicting information about a particular food…this week it was healthy. Last week it would kill you.

It shouldn't be that way! God wants us to be healthy and feel good, so we can do what we need to do when He calls us to do it. He wants us to have our full destinies, but good Christians are limiting their own ability to do so, and often even dying before that can happen.

I've seen fathers that just want to play with their kids again, and they can't because their health issues are standing in the way. You've got parents dying before they're able to see their grandchildren born, much less watch them get married and start a family. Pastors are at the pulpit and they're living in shame, because they know they're overweight and not being a good example for their flock. Doctors are frustrated because they're telling their patients to lose weight but can't manage to do it themselves.

Good people are unhealthy and overweight, and they feel like they have no way out. They feel trapped and hopeless. That is not God's plan for their life, and it breaks my heart...and I'm sure it breaks His, too.

Experiencing my health crisis made me aware of my bondage I had in my body and the need for this message. There was a time, at my heaviest, when I finally said, *I can't lose weight. I've just got to go ahead and learn to love myself where I'm at, and go forward with life.* Basically, I didn't have a solution and I had given up hope of finding one. I thought I had to accept the weight I was at, and reasoned that I should do so in the name of "loving myself."

Ironically, this was the one area of my life where I was willing to believe that loving myself meant accepting less than what I knew was best for me.

It took a hard lesson to show me that not paying attention to my health came with a high price...it opened the doors to disease, and even if it didn't cut my life short, it was definitely going to lessen my ability to fully enjoy it. It was threatening to cancel God's plans that He had for my ministry, and I wasn't going to allow that. I had too many promises from God concerning my future, and I wanted to see them all fulfilled.

At the very first it confused me why God wouldn't heal me dramatically, instantly, through prayer. I knew prayer worked. I had complete faith and belief. But in His wisdom He chose to heal me in a way that would enable me to share the solution with others, and share it abundantly. And I'm on the right track, because since I have said "yes" I have seen thousands of lives changed! And just like I did at the Prayer House, I now teach them how they can take what they've learned and share it with others.

So now I'm on a mission to help others get healthy, and be the BEST that they can be. I want to minister to them completely: body, soul, and spirit. I want to help people break free of the bondages that are holding them from God's best. I'm passionate about it, because I know that during this season it's my purpose in life.

Right now it is more important for God's people to get healthy than any other time. There are big things to do, and even bigger things coming. We simply must be the healthiest we can be, inside and out, to be properly equipped to do what we need to do for the Kingdom, for our families, and for ourselves. God needs strong warriors!

In the hospital, I was fighting for my life. But I was also fighting for my future grandchildren, and the time I would spend with them. I will tell you now, as I write this today, my health is better than it's been since high school, and I held my first grandchild this year! I've not only gotten my life and my health back, it's better than it was before the illness! How can I not be passionate about telling others? I want this for everyone!

God is good, and He will bring you what you need when you surrender. He cares about the health of our body as much as He cares about the health of our soul and our spirit. After all, He created us as three-part beings: body, soul, and spirit, just as He is a three-part God: Father, Son, and Holy Spirit. This episode taught me that to focus on only two of those parts, the spirit and the soul, is to provide an incomplete ministry. It reminds me of churches that focus on the Father and the Son, but don't really address the Holy Spirit in any depth.

So I really feel like God completed the circle in me, and now it's up to me share it with others. All of it. He had been telling me for some time that my ministry would expand, but I had not known exactly what that meant. Now it is crystal-clear: Breathe Freedom Ministries has grown into a complete ministry, one that serves the entire person.

I sit here today in awe of my mighty God, and how His promises continue to come true. I feel blessed, and I'm overjoyed with where I am right now. My ministry is reborn, my health is renewed, and I stand at the beginning of yet another great adventure.

I know I am exactly where God wants me...I just can't wait to see where we go!

CHAPTER 18

THE FRUIT OF OBEDIENCE

—————⟋⟍—————

This brings us to almost present day, and I hesitate to even write that. Every time I do and the book goes a while without being finished, more incredible stuff happens that needs to go in it! But I need to wrap this up somewhere, so here goes...

We've covered a lot, but I believe there are certain things that are worth repeating. Discoveries that radically changed my life and my walk with God, and hold the power (I believe) to change yours, too:

Anyone can expect to hear the Father's voice. I believe many of us get tripped up because we think it must be an audible voice, heard with our natural ears, like when we're talking to our friend over a cup of coffee. The relationship we're after is not in the natural however...it's in the supernatural. It's in the realm where God dwells, and where He wants to take us; not the realm we were confined to before we became a new person in Jesus Christ.

One of the biggest tools we have to help us in this journey is the baptism of the Holy Spirit. It serves as a bridge between these two realms, between the natural and the supernatural. Please don't get hung up on the terminology, although that is how John the Baptist himself referred to it, saying, "I baptize with water, but there is one who comes after me, greater than me...he will baptize with fire and the Holy Spirit."

This baptism is real, and Biblical, and available to God's children right now. This baptism allows God to come alive in us. In God's eyes, it is what "normal" living should be all about. He wants this for us, desperately, this wonderful baptism that knocks down barriers and opens doors between us and Him.

Jesus' call to believe in Him for salvation is only intended to be the first step of faith, not the complete walk. This first step is crucial, as it takes us literally from death to life. We escape the bondage of the natural, and are reborn into the supernatural. That is why the Bible says the grave has lost its sting, because it holds no power over the man whose Spirit will never die. But unfortunately, it is possible to stop right there, like the believers in Acts 19:2 who had not even discovered there was a Holy Spirit. They had received the fullness of the Holy Spirit within them... they were believers who had been reborn from death into life... but they had no idea what that really meant!

And I could certainly relate, because that's exactly where I was, for many years. I knew I was saved, I had been water-baptized, and I loved Jesus. I knew the Holy Spirit was part of the Trinity, which meant He was God. But I really had no clue that there was more. Not more for me to gain, because when you have the Holy Spirit you have the complete Holy Spirit. But there was more to come alive. There was more joy, more peace, more power. There was true authority over the entire kingdom of darkness. There was true deliverance from demons, not just supernatural patience to be able to endure living with them.

And worst of all, I didn't know that God desperately wanted me to have it.

So for a while, I didn't make it easy for Him. When He first tried to introduce me to the awakened Holy Spirit, I didn't understand everything He was trying to show me, and I was the type of person who would avoid what I didn't understand. But because He is Love, He pursued me, many times over the years, in many different ways. He is madly in love with me, and wanted the Holy Spirit awakened in me more than anything. God is Life itself, and His desire was that I would have the fullness of this life on fire within me.

And eventually, slowly at first, but then in a beautiful rush, the walls came down. The relationship came alive. The supernatural became natural, and the mysteries of God began to come into focus. And once I got a glimpse, a taste...I saw it, and I believed it, and I went after it. And the more I desired, the more He revealed. The more desperate I became, the more there was to discover. I came to realize that "more" is not a fixed amount... you can't ever have it all. Not because He's withholding anything, but just because...there's always more!

Love never runs out.

Today I realize that it doesn't all have to make sense. I am okay with that, with the idea that the unexpected is to be expected. I just obey, and see what He has in mind. Since I truly believe that He is always for me, I don't need to question if what He's doing in the moment makes sense. This has helped me develop a desire to care more about what God thinks of me than what people think of me.

Because sometimes it is confusing. For example, I don't know why healing doesn't always happen. I believe it is His will that all are healed, and I have prayed with many people for many various things, yet sometimes a miracle happens and sometimes it doesn't. I don't know why, and I've tried to stop figuring it out.

I remember Heidi Baker saying, "Sometimes we pray for people who are blind and their eyes are opened, and other times we build houses for the ones who don't get their sight back. We don't understand, but that's okay. Rather than question the ways of the Lord, we just do what we know we're supposed to do, and we leave the rest up to Him."

I have noticed this, though: when someone approaches me in the natural realm and asks me to pray for them for healing, I will always pray; but healing doesn't always happen. However, when God approaches me in the supernatural and tells me to pray for somebody, I know without a doubt a miracle is going to take place. The Bible gives us a standing order to pray, so we should always pray. But the point is, the only thing I can really control is my obedience. When I hear God, I act without hesitation. What happens after that is completely up to Him.

I was on the phone with a lady I had only met one time. She was in another part of the country, and I forget what we were originally talking about. But as the conversation went on, God broke in and specifically told me I was to pray for her belly. I had no clue what this meant, but I told her, "God says I need to pray for your belly, is that okay?"

I forget what I prayed, and it really doesn't matter. I just prayed whatever God laid on my heart, and we went on with our conversation. A few days later, this lady contacted me and told me she had experienced a constant pain in her stomach for the last twenty years, and dozens of doctors had not been able to diagnose or correct it. It was something she had just learned to live with…but within a day of our prayer the pain left and had not returned.

I don't know why she suffered for twenty years. She was a Christian and I'm certain she and many other people had prayed for this pain to leave during all this time. I don't know why God chose me, and I don't know what was special about that moment in time when we were on the phone. There are many things I don't know, but I do know this: when I heard the specific command of God, I acted immediately, and I knew it was done.

For me, hearing that voice is the most important thing in my life…I wouldn't want to go a minute without it. The baptism of the Holy Spirit and fire may not be required for salvation, but I believe it is absolutely necessary in order for me to fulfill my earthly ministry, and the destiny He has for me.

So I truly thank God for the day I got desperate. Desperate to know truth. From that day forward my life has not been the same. I feel like that was the moment my spiritual life began, when God called me into everything I was supposed to be. What He created me for, the reason He knit me together in my mother's womb, the victories He called me to before time began, started on that day, in that moment.

In that cry of desperation.

Since that time, everything that God reveals makes life more full, more complete, more satisfying than it was before. As the relationship grows, it not only grows up, into bigger and better things, but it also grows down, into deeper and richer things.

The discovery of true two-way communication with the Father through the Holy Spirit has taught me, among other things, that God is a gentleman. He waits on me; He opens the door and holds it for me. On the road of life, He drives, but He asks me where I would like to go. He never tells me I have to go. He never forces me to do or say something I choose not to. He never violates my free will, because He wants me to do the things He asks out of love, and love is not love unless it's a choice.

As I grew closer to God, as my understanding of who He was grew, it drove me to want to be more obedient. At first, I had to push myself, because obedience didn't always feel good. It wasn't always easy, or convenient, or comfortable. But after doing it a few times, and seeing the fruit and the peace that came with it, I was hooked!

Once I saw, or rather felt, the wonderful presence that it brought, the closeness, the love...my obedience was no longer an issue. The issue then became praying for Him to give me more opportunities to serve, to participate in His plan. No longer did I second-guess myself, and question whether what I heard made sense. I simply said yes, and thanked Him for the fruit I knew was coming.

Well...most of the time. (I did mention earlier I'm still learning, right?)

Recently God told my husband and me to sell our home. We knew He meant right then, but for many reasons we delayed. Our daughter was getting married, other things were going on, I was still in the process of healing, and I was just all around stressing about whether I should handle the sale myself or hire a realtor. I still have an active realtor license, and I felt like I should put it to use, but every time I would think about handling the thousand details I would just shut down.

So eventually, after several months of delaying, I finally got around to obedience. I hired a realtor to list our home, and it was on the market for just a few weeks...and the corona virus hit. All of a sudden, the world was locked down, and the whole process of selling our house suddenly became nowhere near as quick, simple, or profitable as it would have been if I had obeyed completely, immediately.

People can look at this in many ways. Some would say He was punishing me for not being obedient right away, but I don't agree with that...mainly because I know His heart. I look at it as He was trying to bless me, and protect me. He was allowing me to benefit from His knowledge of perfect timing. The outbreak of the corona virus and the shutdown of the entire American economy may have taken all of us by surprise, but trust me, God saw it coming. He was choosing to share that with me because of His great love for me. In the end, it still worked out...we sold our house. But I believe it wasn't as perfect as could have been, had we done it a few months earlier.

God's call to obedience is always for us. Sometimes quick obedience is needed because of what others will do, or simply because God knows what's coming. So my obedience may actually be about me blessing someone else, or it may be about God setting me up to be blessed. Either way, it's for my good.

It can be difficult to pause, and rest, and just be patient. I remember years ago my neighbor was convinced, and told me so, that I was being an irresponsible parent for knowing I was going to lose my house in less than a month and not having a plan for where my family would go. And everything within me, in the natural, agreed with her. But God didn't. He was talking to me, the entire time, assuring me that He had a place for us, and in the right time He would make it known.

So I had to make a conscious decision to trust Him and stand on His words. I had to resist every urge within me that wanted to make plans, find a way, do something...when He was telling me to pause. No matter how it looked to other people, in my heart I knew I was being responsible, because I was obeying God. It was so awesome the next month, literally days before we had to be out of our home, when my friend Traci came and told me about the additional apartment on her property we could move into, completely free until we got back on our feet. Come on, God! You are amazing! (And thanks, Traci!)

Obedience bears wonderful fruit, and some of the sweetest comes from how we handle our tithes.

Growing up I knew that tithing meant I paid 10% to my church. To this day I still firmly believe in financially supporting whatever church or ministries are nourishing me spiritually. Having been in ministry, I realize this is how a ministry survives. But I also noticed that I had always looked at tithing as an automatic thing, an amount that went to the church without any thought behind it; like a bill that was automatically deducted from my check without me even thinking about it.

Looking at it this way was robbing me and other people of a lot of blessings. When I found myself in a place where I was having conversations with God every hour of every day, about every imaginable subject under the sun, it only became natural for me to ask, *God, how much do you want me to give, and where would you like this money to go? What are your plans for this money?*

Sure enough, the Lord has told us to support a congregation we are currently attending. But He also adds in other things to do with money and the amount can vary. Sometimes He tells us to give to a friend we haven't talked to in many years. Sometimes He'll tell us to take someone out to eat. Sometimes He'll have us buy a specific something and take it to someone. Sometimes He will want us to give it anonymously, and sometimes He wants us to tell the person that God highlighted them to us, and it was God's idea. God knows the exact details of each situation, and how our money will do the most good. How it will best accomplish His purposes.

Not only is it wonderful to see the fruit that comes from this, it also makes it so much stinking fun to give! There's nothing like being able to help other people without any strings attached. There's nothing like hearing the stories people share when He tells you to direct an exact amount of money to a certain person at a certain time. We have had people tell us they were praying for that specific amount, right down to the dollar! That type of confirmation of clearly hearing God never happened when our giving was set on automatic.

My husband and I always go to Him and ask where the money should go. It's such an exciting, enjoyable time, especially when we're dealing with a large amount. The more money we give, the more fun God can have! In our mind, He's not "owed" ten percent, and we don't limit Him to ten percent...it's all open to Him. And whatever He says, we're obedient.

But let me tell you where I got tripped up one time: the Lord told me to give the money to one of my children, and I immediately got all in my head...*Is this me saying this? Do I want to give this to my child, because I know they need it, or is this really God telling me this?*

And thankfully, God straightened me out pretty quick. He said, *Misty, stop...are you telling me I don't love your child? I don't want to bless your child? Are you telling me I can give money to your neighbor, but it's not okay for me to give money to your child?*

Oh, God...I'm so sorry...of course you can bless my child...

One specific time He told me to set some money aside for my son, Sam. He continued telling me to do this for many weeks. I kept putting it aside, and it eventually grew to about $1200 before He told me to stop. I let it sit there, because even though God had told me it was for Sam, He didn't tell me to give it to him. We went on with blessing other people out of other checks, and just kind of forgot about the money. After some time, about four months, an expense came up with Sam's college that he wasn't expecting. As soon as I heard about it, I already knew how much it was going to be…and sure enough, it was right at $1200! *Way to go, God!*

At that point we were able to share with our son that God had us putting money for him to the side for some time, and it had been sitting there waiting for this exact moment. I even showed him where I had actually written this in my journal when we first started saving. It was beautiful, because not only did it free Sam from the burden of a huge expense, but he was also able to see that this money was directly from God to him personally, out of His love and foreknowledge of what was coming.

Remember talking earlier about how obedience puts us in a position where God can bless us? Any normal time a $1200 unexpected expense would not be a happy thing. But this day was turned to great celebration, simply because we had followed His lead!

Other times God has told us to give something away instead of sell it. When we were moving we had a washer and dryer we didn't need, and we were going to put them up for sale. Immediately God highlighted our daughter and her husband to us, and told us we should give them to them instead. When we contacted her, she was almost speechless. After a minute of, "Really? Really?" she let us know that for the last three weeks their washer had been leaking and they were currently saving up to get a new one. We didn't know about this problem they were having…but God did!

Once we allow ourselves the freedom to let God decide where

and how and how much we give, we are given the opportunity to take part in the amazing things He has planned. He shows us a glimpse of what's on His mind, what His priorities are. And we can't out-give God! When we give to others, He gives right back. Recently the Lord placed it in my heart to help someone through my business even though they couldn't afford it, and within 24 hours I had received so much other new business it was crazy. It was like the dam burst, and all these blessings came pouring in.

It's almost as if it works every time, like it's a law of the Kingdom or something...

CHAPTER 19

ROADBLOCKS

In order to learn, and grow, and become spiritually mature, it takes action. It requires stepping out, moving forward.

As we do, it's important for us to identify roadblocks. The largest and strongest of these are not in our circumstances, the things around us. While things like peer pressure and seemingly hopeless financial challenges can be difficult to overcome, the toughest roadblocks are always found within our own minds. After all, that's where the true battle is taking place.

The enemy knows us pretty well, and as such he knows right where to place things to trip us up. If they were in the middle of the road with orange stripes painted on them, they would be easy to spot. But most of the time they're not...they're buried deep, hidden among lies and firmly-held beliefs we picked up somewhere along the way. Many times we aren't even aware of them.

With me, a big roadblock was the religious spirit. Oh, I still get hit with it, sometimes when I least expect it, but thankfully now it has a yucky feeling I can recognize almost immediately. This book is not intended to come against traditional religion, except where traditional religion holds back our spiritual walk and growth. It's a great reminder that Jesus' largest fight was against religion and religious people. Think about it: He defeated the devil, defeated sin, defeated death...but religion tried to kill Him.

This reminds me how nasty the religious spirit can be, and if religion, legalism, and tradition are keeping me from truth and love, I want to be rid of them. The sooner I allow God to identify it and deal with it, the sooner I can move into His truth and His plan.

Speaking in tongues was a huge roadblock for me. I had grown up in churches that did not talk about speaking in tongues, so by default I was pretty much against the whole thing. Even later on when I began devouring my Bible on my own, and I was reading with a new understanding, I still maintained this irrational block against the entire idea. I thought the whole thing was only for times past, not something happening today.

But, thankfully, eventually, I began to chase after truth. I relentlessly asked the Father, once I was confident I could hear His voice, to please reveal truth. I was certain when it came to being a Christian, there was more than I was currently experiencing. I kept thinking of Moses, and all he did, and I realized there was no way he could have done those things without a level of power far beyond anything I was walking in. And I wanted to know, *How was that possible? What did he have that I didn't have?*

I knew there was power there somewhere, and I was trying to find that power. And the thing I kept landing on was this: Moses had face-to-face communication with God. That's what

I was after. I certainly wasn't on a quest to speak in tongues; I really didn't even believe in it. I wanted that face-to-face communication. I desired that level of communion, that degree of intimacy. I knew it was possible between God and man, and I knew I didn't have it.

And I allowed that to begin to bother me.

Looking back, I can see that this blockage I had formed in my mind against speaking in tongues had been stopping me from moving forward. Not the fact that I didn't speak in tongues, but the fact I was so irrationally against it. That blockage in my mind needed to be torn down before I could advance to the next level in my relationship with God. For me, based on some reasoning I had formed long ago and was unwilling to question, speaking in tongues was a non-negotiable. It was a belief I was holding on to so strongly that the enemy was able to use it as a major roadblock in my relationship with God. It was the one thing that, for whatever reason, was a hang-up of mine and stood in the way of me reaching my real goal: face-to-face communication.

I mean, think about it: I had read an entire book I knew was from God, because it was speaking directly to the Holy Spirit within me, making it come alive and jump in a way that it never had before. But sure enough, as soon as the book mentioned tongues, I dropped it without a second thought. I was ready to throw away all the wonders that were contained in the previous chapters because, *Sorry, I just can't go there.*

I had hit my roadblock. End of the line.

Thank God (literally, thank God) the Lord clearly spoke to me and told me to pick it back up and keep going. Otherwise I would still be stuck right where I was: a Christian deeply in love with God, but wondering where the power was…wondering where the true victory was…wondering where the more was.

I have since come into the understanding that praying in the Spirit (speaking in tongues) is one of the most powerful tools I have as a Christian. When I'm happy, I sing in tongues and my Spirit soars. When I'm sad, I cry out in tongues and I know God hears the depth of my pain. When I am scared, praying in tongues will calm me, and during those times when I just don't know what to pray, I can always pray in tongues and He will give me understanding and reveal truth. I can trust that when my Spirit talks directly to the Spirit of God, He perfectly understands.

I bring this up not as a defense of tongues, but simply because every one of us probably has a silly little thing. When you get down to it, this is the very nature of spiritual warfare. This is how the devil can convince me to do or not do something, by having me believe or not believe something. If he doesn't want me to go somewhere and meet a certain group of people, he probably won't cause my car not to start. That would just make me want to get there even more. But if he can convince me in my mind that those people don't like me, for whatever reason…I'm less likely to go anywhere near them.

Again, the true battle is in the mind.

So it's important to continually ask myself, *Do I have a mental roadblock? Is there a belief or emotion that is keeping me from the incredible next step that God has for me?* If so, I need to confront it, and with prayer push through it. I always trust that my loving Father will meet me on the other side.

For me it hasn't only been tongues. I've had issues with healing, and holy laughter, and seeing someone fall out on the floor under the power of the Holy Spirit. All of these things had a lot of traditional religious beliefs coming against them that made me uneasy for quite some time. I eventually learned to just give them to God, and allow Him to decide where He stood on them, rather than me judging them for Him.

Since then, I've been in many services where people fall out when the Holy Spirit hits them, and I've remained standing. But I've also been hit by the Holy Spirit so hard I have fallen while others have remained standing. I remember a friend being overcome by holy laughter one time, before it had happened to me, and I actually got irritated at her because she wouldn't quit laughing! I mean, it seemed like days! I was thinking, *Okay, I get it. You're happy. Get ahold of it, already.*

Then a few months later it hit me for the first time, and I tell you what…when the Father finally hit me with that God-sized portion of joy, there was no getting around it. I started laughing and simply could not stop. It wasn't that things were funny, it's just that they were…so incredibly good. There was such a purity to the laughter. And finally, I realized why my friend had been laughing…she had no other choice! Her spirit was being soaked in a joy and a goodness so deep that it had no option but to bubble over into laughter.

So today I look at it like this: at different times God will fill us to overflowing with different things. It might be faith, which allows us to persevere in the darkest of circumstances; or courage, which enables us to fight beyond what we thought possible; or grace, which allows us the ability to forgive the seemingly unforgivable.

How beautiful is that?

The more I work with God to remove my roadblocks, the closer our relationship becomes. I reach a point where I'm just walking and talking with Him all day long. The Bible instructs me to pray without ceasing, and truly the smallest portion of my prayer involves stopping, and closing my eyes, and praying in the traditional sense. A large part comes when I'm just driving, and walking, and talking, and doing whatever.

If I'm thinking about something, I'm asking God what He thinks about it. Every decision, large and small, gets discussed with Him. Every joy. Every concern. And I am always actively listening for His interruption...which He does quite frequently. In fact, some of the most wonderful rewards of listening to God come when I allow myself the freedom to change my plans right on the spot, based on what He says.

Once I realized I didn't necessarily have to get "on my knees" to pray, that it didn't have to be an official act, our relationship really took off. Now please know, there are still times I find myself on my knees, but traditions and my religious understanding no longer dictate what prayer should look like. I had to break out of that shell to find the freedom to recognize prayer for what it is, which is more like hanging out with a best friend. I realize He's God and I'm not, but that doesn't mean there needs to be some great distance between us...especially when He desires this wonderful closeness more than anything.

I always knew that I wanted more of God...but it was exciting to realize that God wants more of me!

My relationship with God isn't required to follow any particular formula. I get to experience God in whatever way He wants me to. I don't have to pass this test and reach that qualification in order to have a deep, close, personal experience. In fact, I'm not required to do anything, and our relationship is not required to look like any particular thing. Just as every single relationship between people is different, every relationship someone has with God will be different. Some of the things He and I do, and some of the ways He communicates with me, I've never seen anyone else experience. It's our thing. That's what makes it special!

So in our individual relationships with God, what might be right for some people may not be right for others. If God is truly talking to each one of us, individually, it won't look like we're all listening to the same recording, hearing the same thing. Some things in the Spirit are similar, but each relationship will be unique. That's why I can't tell you what your relationship with Him will look like. I can't write a book on what your relationship with Him will be. I can only tell you about what mine is.

Really coming to understand that there truly is no formula, that God will communicate with each of us differently, has helped me to not judge others. I no longer believe there's any certain "mold" that Christians need to fit into.

In fact, growing up spiritually, becoming mature, required me to let go of tradition. I learned the Holy Spirit is very non-traditional, and He wants to move in my life in a very non-traditional way. Whatever pre-arranged rules I may have about how the things of God are supposed to look and feel will only stifle that. His movement will be restricted, and our relationship will not go to the depths God wants it to.

Seriously, the last thing the Holy Spirit needs is me telling Him what the rules of the relationship are.

Rules in and of themselves are not bad things. Rules are meant to protect us. For example, many leaders preach against alcohol, that drinking is something that should not be done at all. I believe that rule was put in place to protect against drunkenness, which is something the Bible warns against, as well as to protect others who may have a problem with alcohol, so that I don't cause them to falter by drinking around them. That's a good and reasonable rule, as it lines up with Jesus' command to love others as we love ourselves.

But it's also a rule that, in my opinion, has a particular application. I believe for someone who doesn't have an issue with alcohol, and avoids drunkenness, an occasional drink could be okay. They don't need a rule to protect them if they have the right heart and intent. I believe God is against drunkenness, and against us being a stumbling block to others, not against a glass of wine. There is good and bad in everything. In the Bible, Timothy is told to use wine as medicine. In other areas we are told to not have too much wine, or to not drink at all in certain leadership positions. I truly believe it's between you and God.

When I recognize and follow God's original intention, which is always love for others and love for myself, there are definite fruits that result in my life. These include joy, peace, patience, kindness, goodness, faithfulness, gentleness, and self-control. The presence of these fruits in my life tells me I am on the right track to a closer relationship with God. It tells me that I am living my life from a position of love, which is better than a position of just following all the rules.

I used to think God stood in heaven wagging His finger at me, pointing out what I did wrong. I remember when I was younger, sitting in church with such shame and guilt. When I knew I had made bad choices in my life, I felt like the best thing for me to do was hide from God and give Him a chance to get over His anger.

But once I really got to know God, on a relationship basis, I realized that when I come to Him with my sin and a repentant heart, He is quick to open His arms and say, *Come to me, my child.* He'll hug me, and pat me on the back, and give me a little time to heal, before He turns me around and says *Okay, let's try again...go ahead, you got this!* He never sits me down to review the rules with me and show me where I messed up.

He is such a loving Father. He knows exactly when to sit and listen, and exactly when to pat me on the back, and even when it's time to push me forward. He knows better than I do, because He knows things I don't even know about myself, and He knows the future! So over time it became easier to understand that the best thing I could do—always—was run as fast as I could into His arms. He doesn't want me to hide in my shame and guilt; what He wants is to dust me off, and wipe my tears, and love on me.

God is always for me. God is never against me. His desire is always to bless me, to protect me, to love on me. He is always looking for that special way to communicate how precious I am to Him, and just how much He loves me. Which brought us to a time, a few years back, when He interrupted my thoughts as I was driving across the Sunshine Skyway Bridge. I was way up at the peak, hundreds of feet above Tampa Bay, looking out at the sunrise.

Trust and breathe, He whispered.

I didn't know why He was telling me this, but I immediately declared, *Lord, I trust you completely.*

So breathe...

I began to breathe, slow relaxing breaths as I crested the hill and headed down the other side. Several slow, deep breaths.

Now...Give your car to Allie.

My immediate thought was, *Lord, what?! How will I get anoth...oh, yeah...*I just continued to breathe. I was in no position to purchase another car right then, but I just chose to trust, rather than question anything. I was certain there would be a time in the future when this would be doable, and I wouldn't be left without a—

Do it today, He said.

Oh, boy! Breathe! Breathe! Breathe-breathe…breathe…okay…

Then, a beautiful thing happened. The less I thought about how this might affect me, the more I began to get excited. God wanted Allie blessed with a car! My daughter was on His mind, and He wanted to do something special for her! How awesome was that?

I drove straight home, and as I was gathering together all the paperwork, I also realized the special thing He had just done for me. Twenty-four years earlier I had been amazed by Laurie's relationship with God, and the fact that she heard Him and completely trusted Him to the point she would give away her car. And now, in a way that He knew would mean everything to me, God was reminding me of how far our relationship had come, and how pleased He was with me. He even chose to do it while I was driving over a bridge, just like when Laurie's friend's car broke down.

And you know what? God always trades up. We don't give to get, but that doesn't change the fact that God always wants better for us, and when we align our steps with His we will see tremendous fruit in our lives. I could hardly wait for Allie to get home so I could give away my car, and in a very short time God replaced it with another one, better than I ever imagined.

CHAPTER 20

STRUT YOUR FEATHERS

———————— ⁊ ————————

I know that God has a plan for me.

I have a definite destiny, and He created me with that destiny already in His mind. Not only that, but from the very beginning He gave me everything I need, within me, to be able to fulfill that destiny. He already knows the fullness of who I am, even though I don't...and that's what this journey is about.

Every step I take deeper into this relationship, closer to Him, reveals one more part of me to myself. Sometimes it's something beautiful that He sees in me, and I stand amazed at who I am in His eyes. Sometimes it's something not so lovely, and without condemnation He and I work through it together. Sometimes it's something big and powerful, and I am shocked at His confidence in my capabilities. But no matter what it is, it's always wrapped in His love, and it's always an incredible blessing.

When we receive the Holy Spirit, at salvation, we receive everything God has for us, in terms of who we are. We don't receive the Holy Spirit a little bit, and it grows. The Holy Spirit is fully God, and when we have the Holy Spirit we have all of God living within us. So why would we think that we wouldn't be able to feel, sense, and hear Him? That was the plan all along! He's just waiting for us to fully awaken to it.

It took me quite a while, but I finally began to realize who I truly was, and what I had within me. I remember Andrew Wommack saying one time, "I have nothing more in me than what you have. I just know what I have."

I finally realized it does not make me prideful to think that I am special...because I really am. I'm special because He made me unique, and there is no one else out there like me. And what's more, I house the Living God within my body...the power that created the universe is within me. The love that is the very meaning of Love is within me. That's pretty special!

I have a dear friend named Pam who gave me a word from the Lord recently. "Misty," she said, "This season of your life you are to strut your feathers. Just like a peacock."

At first I thought...*Oh my goodness, that's prideful, I can't do that!*

But then truth came in, and I realized it's not my feathers I'm strutting...it's what God has created in me, and showing off these feathers is only going to highlight Him! Think about it: we are beautiful. We are made beautiful. We are in the image of Him. Why would we not walk and feel that way, and show His beautiful colors?

Along with my destiny, my passion and my purpose are also within me, since the beginning. When I'm not feeling fulfilled, it's likely because I'm not watering the things God placed within me that have such a strong need to grow. When I am feeding these things, there is a joy within me that feels so good, and so right, and so fulfilling, that whatever I'm doing is not even a job anymore. I'm able to pour so much more time and love into it because I get so much more out of it. I was made for it, and it satisfies me deep inside like nothing else can.

This doesn't even have to be a ministry position. I don't have to be a pastor, or a missionary, or own a non-profit. I could be a doctor, or a lawyer, or a teacher, or a scientist, or a carpenter. That incredible joy can be found in any of these things if it's a part of my destiny. It doesn't matter what it is…all that matters is that I find it. When I do, the feeling is unmistakable and irreplaceable. I have learned to search for that beautiful feeling until I find it, and this helps me to know exactly where God wants me to be.

My fulfillment is very important to God. I mean, He has given me everything…he has placed Himself within me…it's not selfish for me to want joy. I am Joy. It's not ridiculous for me to expect love, and to love. I have Love itself living inside of me. I have every reason to expect peace in my life. My Lord, who lives in me, is Peace.

The actual path to my destiny, however, can be very curvy. Sometimes this is from me being off course, and sometimes it's by His design. There are experiences He needs me to go through in order to make me stronger, but there are also experiences I put myself through that He will use to strengthen me. These might not have been His doing, His plan for my life, but I've found that He doesn't waste an opportunity. A favorite pastor of mine said, "God doesn't cause everything, but He also doesn't waste anything."

That's such a wonderful way to look at it, and it helps keep me from beating myself up over my mistakes. It also helps me not to question circumstances, things over which I have no control. The fact is, God has a plan for everything, and the things that weren't part of His plan He will work in somehow. Every scrape of my knee and every tough time is going to have some benefit down the road, along the way to my destiny.

I had a really beautiful friend with a beautiful heart, who loved the Lord dearly. He had grown up with money, and when I would talk about difficulties other people were going through, he sometimes had a tough time comprehending that struggle. It certainly wasn't wrong for him to be in the position he was in, and God was using him to do great things in many areas. But it reminded me that sometimes living through a certain situation does allow me to relate better to others in the same boat.

Looking back on the financial struggle my husband and I went through when the kids were young, I see now that it really grew me as a person. It brought Joe and I closer in many different ways, and it brought me into a better understanding of the situations that good, hard-working people can sometimes find themselves in. It changed a lot of my mindsets, and I am thankful for that.

In fact, Joe and I both look back at that time as a blessing. I remember him having a conversation one December with our teenage daughter, and asking her what she thought about the previous year. She mentioned all the highlights, all the fun things she had done, at which point my husband told her, "We have just come through what will probably be the worst financial season of our entire life. Always remember that your happiness is not dependent on money."

So this road to my destiny has hills, and valleys, and curves. Sometimes it's paved and sometimes it's not. Nevertheless, it's a good road. It's my road. It's important that I remove any roadblocks and keep moving along it. Because every valley I go through, I come out the other side stronger, and wiser, and better equipped to help more people. Sometimes by my experience, sometimes by my knowledge, or sometimes simply by my testimony.

One time in prayer I went before the Lord and specifically asked Him to show me my destiny. To show me what I was created to be. He showed me His vision of me, through His eyes:

I was carrying a torch of His truth, and going around the world starting fires. He told me, *You were created to bring Light into the darkness. You were created to bring the truth of who I am to others, to reveal my character, and the ways in which I love them. And you were created to reveal the truth of who they are, so they can grow into the person they were created to be.*

Wow. That is huge, and that's my hope for this book, and for you. That the truth of who God is will come alive within you, and that you will know the truth of who you are in His eyes. This book has a purpose. God asked me to write it, it's not something that I necessarily wanted to do. He asked me to be vulnerable, to put into words things I would otherwise have kept private. It's all about getting the truth out. I was somebody who didn't know truth for so long, but desired to be a good girl, desired to be right with the Lord, to be a good person.

I didn't know what I didn't know. But now that I do, I have to share it.

But I will say, when He asked me to write a book, I said, *God are you kidding?*

You have to understand, this is the one thing I'm horrible at...I've never been good with writing, or with words. In fact, I have a habit of mangling words so bad, my friends have even developed a name for the jumbled-up concoctions that sometimes come out of my mouth. They call them "Misty-isms." They make perfect sense to me, but usually leave other people confused or cracking up.

But God said, many times, *It is important—I need you to get it done.* And this has been one of the largest stretches I've ever gone through, this time of laying everything wide open. But in that stretching, I know I'm growing. This process is going to help me as much as I pray it helps other people. I trust that He will grow me in ways I could never imagine. By Him stretching me, and making me uncomfortable at times, I am growing into the person He already sees me as.

There have always been things I desired to do, but didn't feel like I could. Allowing Him to stretch me in little bitty steps is growing me into the best Misty I can possibly be. These are not just fluff words; for the first time in my life, I have so much freedom. So much confidence. I still have areas we're working on, of course. I hope He's never completely finished, at least not while I'm on this earth. As much as looking back makes me smile, looking ahead is even more exciting. There's so much more to go!

I realize that when it comes to my spiritual growth, God doesn't expect me to have a plan, but rather just to listen to Him and let Him lead. When I allow Him to freely move and do what He wants in my life, I have His favor, and miraculous things can happen. At that point I am moving with Him in the supernatural, in the realm where miracles are birthed. When I try to figure it all out, and apply my natural understanding, I've just limited myself to the natural. I've restricted His free movement in my life.

And at that point it becomes my job to worry about everything, and make sure it all works out. All the obstacles become my responsibility! Who wants that? Besides, the things I see as obstacles are not obstacles to God, and the path He wants me to take is often not the obvious one. So it works a lot better when I give the driving back to Him. This is where the stretching comes in.

Hearing my Father's voice allows me to not focus on a million other things, and instead put all of my focus on Him. Even though there are many, many steps to this journey, I no longer have to focus on every single one. I just need to be available to hear Him. I just need to show up! The how's and the why's and the if's are His to focus on, not mine.

A good example is leading someone to the Lord. That conversation is different every time…it's not a script that I have memorized. What I do is listen to God in the moment, and follow His lead. After all, their salvation is not my responsibility, it's God's responsibility. My responsibility is to listen to Him and follow His direction, which is different every time.

When it comes to deliverance, there's no set formula for that either. There's no step-by-step plan that works every time, other than showing up and listening to God, and allowing Him to lead us. We do our part and let Him do His part, because after all He is the Light, and Light is the only thing that chases out darkness.

While I desired to hear God's voice and receive the baptism of the Holy Spirit, and prayed diligently for each of them, it wasn't my efforts that made them happen. My responsibility was to allow myself to become desperate for whatever He had for me, whatever He wanted to tell me. My job was to finally reach the point where I stopped debating in my head about what was "of God" and what wasn't, and just allow the Holy Spirit to do what He wanted to do all along.

When I'm listening to and following the voice of God, I don't need to worry whether what I did was right, or best, or even what to do next. I don't need to question why I am taking this path instead of that one. The path I am called to follow is to grow in the things of the Spirit. That's it. Everything else is left to God, and when I do that everything else miraculously falls into place. Not meaning I don't have direction in my life, or have dreams and desires, but simply that I'm allowing His hand to be on the rudder.

One thing I know is that along the way things are going to constantly change. It's not up to me to see them coming, or guess what happens next. My only end goal is a more complete, more alive, more exciting walk with God. I trust that He will give me the wisdom and discernment to grow in spiritual maturity. I just need to make sure that I'm not holding on to anything that would hinder His ability to move me along.

This singular focus on God is the only thing that will bring true fulfillment into my life. Fulfillment in the true sense, as in lacking nothing, being completely satisfied. Everything else will eventually leave me empty, causing me to jump from one thing to another looking to find meaning and purpose. But walking and talking with God is completely fulfilling, every day. Fresh every morning...actually fresh every conversation!

As I remain in His presence, I remain in His rest. That doesn't mean I'm not doing hard work and taking actions, but rather that I'm doing it with Him, through His power. And I have true joy, and true fulfillment, and true peace, in a measure and purity that I cannot find anywhere other than with Him. I know that I am home.

As wonderful as all that sounds, here's the really exciting part: God has told me over and over there is someone out there who needs to hear this, needs to know this. Someone is searching for answers and this book is going to allow them to understand, stretch, and grow into more than they ever imagined.

There's absolutely nothing different or more special about me. I'm the same as you, and you, and you. What made the change in my life is that I saw that there was more and I believed I could have it. I got desperate and went after it. That's it.

So while I didn't know what I didn't know, the fact is that I still don't. But I know what I know, and I know this is real. I know that the closer I get to God, the more mysteries are revealed. I know that just as surely as when I accepted Jesus Christ my life was saved, when I experienced the baptism of the Holy Spirit and fire, my eyes were opened to my destiny and calling. And I know God wants everyone to be in their destiny. This is His plan for all of His children, and has been from the beginning. Ever since He walked and talked with Adam in the garden, and they experienced that incredible closeness, there has been a plan to restore what was lost. Salvation…God placing Himself inside of us…is that plan. The baptism of the Holy Spirit and fire brings it to fruition.

It is again possible to walk, and talk, with God!

If you think God might have had you in mind when I wrote this book, then I say please jump in! He is ready, and waiting, with so many treasures He has wanted to give you for so very long.

Don't worry about figuring it out. He will guide you, all along the way. If you step off the path, He'll gently nudge you back on. He is such a beautiful lead. He's such a wonderful tour guide. This whole entire journey, your loving Father will be right there to help you get exactly where you need to go, exactly when you need to get there.

All you need to do is step out, and take action. Tell Him you're ready for more. If you're unsure, go ahead and ask God.

He won't be offended…in fact He will be delighted at your newfound curiosity, and your willingness to leave truth in His hands. And hey, if you throw in a healthy dose of desperation, you might be amazed at what He answers you with!

Since time began He has waited for this moment.

This very moment. He has waited for you, for the relationship to be fully restored to His vision of how He knows it can be. There truly is no more time to stand and debate it. As His child, your heavenly Father wants to give you the supernatural power you need to live this new life.

For those who ask will receive, and those who seek will find, and the door will be opened to anyone who knocks…If you, then…know how to give good gifts to your children, how much more will your Father in heaven give the Holy Spirit to those who ask Him!

Luke 11:10,13 NIV

God always honors His Word; believe it!

SALVATION PRAYER

———

Jesus died so that you and I do not have to.

While our physical bodies will pass away, when we accept Christ's free gift of salvation the Holy Spirit will come to live within us, and our spirits will not die.

If you want to receive God's free gift of salvation, simply believe in your heart, and speak this prayer out loud:

"Jesus, I confess that You are my Lord and Savior. I believe in my heart that God raised You from the dead. By faith in Your Word, I receive salvation now. Thank You for saving me!"

It's that simple! Your spirit is sealed for eternity in the presence of God. You are a brand new you!

What you just prayed has sealed your eternal fate. Your spirit will not experience death. But God, our loving Father, has so much more prepared for us. Living with Him is not just about escaping death...it's about truly living life!

BAPTISM OF THE HOLY SPIRIT PRAYER

God wants you to experience all of Him. If you are ready to experience the MORE, then you are ready to receive the baptism of the Holy Spirit (and fire). This prayer will invite the complete activation of the Holy Spirit to come alive within you. All you have to do is ask, believe, and receive! Pray out loud:

"Father, I recognize my need for your power to live this new life. Holy Spirit I give you permission to activate and fill every area of my being. By faith, I receive the baptism of the Holy Spirit and fire right now! Thank you for baptizing me. Holy Spirit, you are welcome in my life."

Congratulations! Now you're filled with God's supernatural power. If a language you don't recognize rises up from within your heart, allow it to come through your mouth. As you do this, you will be releasing God's power from within and building yourself up in the Spirit. You can do this whenever and wherever you like.

It doesn't really matter whether you felt anything at this moment or not when you prayed. If you believed in your heart that you received, then God's Word promises you did.

Forget the former things;
do not dwell on the past.

See, I am doing
a new thing!

Now it springs up;
do you not perceive it?

I am making a way
in the wilderness and
streams in the wasteland.

ISAIAH 43:18-19 NIV

ABOUT THE AUTHOR

MISTY STINSON is an ordained minister who loves people and loves Jesus. Her joy in life is coaching others to live in freedom—body, soul, and spirit. She believes that truth brings healing, and healing allows people to live and walk in their full destiny and purpose.

Misty and her husband currently travel the US, where she ministers to people who are desiring more of God. She focuses on teaching others to hear God's voice, helping them discover who He is, and uncovering His divine purpose for their life. Misty is living her best life and wants the same for everyone!

MINISTRIES OVER THE YEARS

2010: Co-founded Selah Freedom, a non-profit that helps survivors of human trafficking re-establish their lives.

2015: Founded Breathe Freedom Ministries, a non-profit that empowers and educates those desiring to live a victorious life with power, truth, and purpose.

2018: Founder and CEO, Live In Freedom, LLC, a business that specializes in weight loss, health, nutrition, and coaching.

CONTACT

If you have any questions or if you prayed a prayer from this book, reach out to us through our website so we can celebrate and help you with your new journey. MistyStinson.com

www.ingramcontent.com/pod-product-compliance
Lightning Source LLC
Chambersburg PA
CBHW051416090426
42737CB00014B/2702